Offshoring of
American Jobs

Offshoring of American Jobs

What Response from U.S. Economic Policy?

Jagdish Bhagwati and
Alan S. Blinder

The Alvin Hansen
Symposium on Public
Policy
Harvard University

edited and with an
introduction by
Benjamin M. Friedman

The MIT Press
Cambridge, Massachusetts
London, England

For information about special quantity discounts, please email special_sales@mitpress.mit.edu

This book was set in Palatino by SNP Best-set Typesetter Ltd., Hong Kong. Printed and bound in the United States of America.

Library of Congress Cataloging-in-Publication Data

Alvin Hansen Symposium on Public Policy (2007 : Harvard University)
Offshoring of American jobs : what response from U.S. economic policy? / Jagdish Bhagwati and Alan S. Blinder ; the Alvin Hansen Symposium on Public Policy, Harvard University ; edited and with an introduction by Benjamin M. Friedman.
    p. cm. — (Alvin Hansen Symposium on Public Policy at Harvard University)
Includes bibliographical references and index.
ISBN 978-0-262-01332-1 (hbk. : alk. paper) 1. Offshore outsourcing—United States. 2. Labor market—United States. 3. Manpower policy—United States. 4. Free trade—United States. I. Bhagwati, Jagdish N., 1934– II. Blinder, Alan S. III. Friedman, Benjamin M. IV. Title.
HD2368.U6A48   2009
331.12'042—dc22

                                                              2009005943

10 9 8 7 6 5 4 3 2 1

In memoriam
Richard A. Musgrave

Contents

Introduction

Benjamin M. Friedman

Many Americans today have the sense that there is something different, and not to the good, about this country's economic relations with the rest of the world. Specifically, many people fear that their economic security—if they are working, their livelihood—is at risk.

Much of this anxiety presumably reflects familiar problems that are now simply occurring in larger magnitude than previously. America's trade imbalance, for example, has become both large and chronic. In 2007 U.S. imports overran U.S. exports by $713 billion, or more than 5 percent of the country's entire economic output—a situation that both our own government and most international financial institutions would quickly label dangerous, even irresponsible, if it occurred anywhere else. Another familiar part of the problem is the financial flows that are the mirror image of this trade deficit. The United States as a whole, including both the government and private firms, is borrowing from abroad and selling assets to foreign buyers far in excess of the pace at which this country is lending to foreigners and buying foreign assets. As the trade deficit persists from year to year, these amounts borrowed, and the assets sold, accumulate. Today America is the world's largest debtor country, even net of foreign assets and debts held here, and the ratio of the country's net debt to its national income continues to rise. Further, the purchase of some specific U.S. assets by foreign interests (the Chinese government's attempt to buy an American oil company, and an Arab investment group's attempt to buy the firm responsible for maintaining security at American ports, to name just two) often triggers political sensitivities beyond the economic implications. Nobody thinks the situation—either the trade deficit or the consequent net borrowing—is good for the country.

But there is also a widespread sense that the situation today, and even more so what may occur in the foreseeable future, are not just more of the same written larger. One new development that makes today's situation at least potentially different is the emergence of China and, more recently, India as major competitors. (Other developing countries are undergoing a similar experience, but they matter less in this context because they are smaller; China and India together have 2.4 billion citizens.) Crudely put, the relevant supply of labor to the integrated world economy has doubled. The supply of factories, machinery, and other productive physical capital has continued to grow, but not nearly in so discontinuous a way. Any standard theory of returns to different factors of production suggests that doubling the supply of labor, while increasing the supply of capital much more modestly, is likely to exert downward pressure on wages for those workers who were already in the integrated world economy. In the United States, wages for most workers have indeed either stagnated or declined, compared to rising prices, in recent years. It is no surprise that many disappointed workers suspect that having to compete against foreign labor, to a far greater extent than was the case not long ago, is part of the reason.

A second new development is that advances in technology have rendered an ever wider range of jobs subject to this international competition. To be sure, it is no more possible to have one's hair cut remotely, or to have a lawn in the United States mown by someone abroad, than before. But ongoing improvements in communications, together with the steady movement of production into service industries, have made it possible—even straightforward—to carry out more and more of a country's economic activity at a distance. Increasing numbers of Americans therefore perceive "offshoring," as the phenomenon has become known, as an actual or potential threat to their jobs, or to their wages even if they hold onto their jobs. The image of computer programmers or call center operators in Bangalore has become just as familiar as that of factory workers in Guangzhou. The consequent threat may be exactly analogous to what workers exposed to international competition have faced for decades (think of the steel industry, for example, or autos, or shipbuilding, or shoe manufacturing), but today whole new groups of Americans feel threatened. And there at least appear to be far more Americans who feel such concerns even if they are not directly at risk.

Two important questions follow. First, does "offshoring" actually represent a new, or different, kind of threat to the livelihood of American workers? Acute fears voiced in the popular media notwithstanding, it is clear that the number of American jobs transferred overseas in this way has been small to date. But will those job losses increase significantly over some future time horizon that matters for today's public policy decisions? Alternatively, even if not a single American job actually moved overseas, would the threat that this might happen enable employers to depress wages significantly below the trajectory they would otherwise follow?

Second, even if the answer is yes on both counts—that American jobs will disappear and wages for American workers who retain their jobs will be depressed—the further question is then how this country's public policy should respond. Are there policy measures that would improve the situation? And improve it for whom? After all, the history of trade policy, in the United States no less than in other countries, is replete with examples of measures either adopted or merely proposed that protect the interests of one or another group at the expense of either someone else or even everyone else. But experience also demonstrates that simply standing back, firmly maintaining the traditional free-trade stance, likewise advantages some of a country's citizens at the expense of others. Much of the debate in this arena is usually about whether the consequent gains to the winners exceed the losses to the losers. But in the absence of measures by which the winners compensate the losers (something that experience shows is at best difficult to arrange politically) or even just some way of directly comparing welfare gains across individuals (a challenge that the discipline of economics abandoned more than a century ago), it is unclear that this is the only, or even the most important, focus of attention.

The papers offered here by Jagdish Bhagwati and Alan S. Blinder, together with the remarks of four commentators, address exactly these important but difficult issues: Is today's situation—in particular, offshoring—different? And if so, who should do what about it? These papers do not come to a consensus; that is not the point of the symposium series of which they were a part. Rather, the object was, and is, to air both sides of key public policy questions, and in a way that is accessible not just to researchers but to students, the policy community, and the interested general public.

These papers and discussions were presented at the fourth Alvin Hansen Symposium on Public Policy, held at Harvard University on May 2, 2007.[1] In introducing these proceedings, I want to express my very sincere personal thanks, as well as the gratitude of the Harvard Economics Department, to Leroy Sorenson Merrifield and the late Marian Hansen Merrifield, together with numerous former students of Alvin Hansen, whose generosity made possible this series of public policy symposia that the Economics Department now sponsors at Harvard in Alvin Hansen's name. Their eager participation in this effort stands as testimony to the profound and positive effect that Professor Hansen had on so many younger economists.

I am also grateful to my colleagues James Duesenberry and Gregory Mankiw, who served with me on the committee that chose the subject for this symposium; to Yvonne Zinfon, who helped arrange the symposium's logistics; to John Covell, for his support in bringing these proceedings to publication; and especially to Jagdish Bhagwati and Alan S. Blinder, as well as our four discussants, for contributing their papers and comments.

James Duesenberry, along with our former colleague Richard Musgrave, also served on the committee that first established the Alvin Hansen Symposium series more than ten years ago. Both were students, colleagues, and ultimately friends of Alvin Hansen. All of us in the Harvard Economics Department were saddened by Richard Musgrave's death just a few months before this symposium took place. This volume is dedicated to his memory.

In 1967, in his eightieth year, Alvin Hansen received the American Economic Association's Francis E. Walker medal. James Tobin, in presenting this award, described him as follows:

Alvin H. Hansen, a gentle revolutionary who has lived to see his cause triumphant and his heresies orthodox, an untiring scholar whose example and influence have fruitfully changed the directions of his science, a political economist who has reformed policies and institutions in his own country and elsewhere without any power save the force of his ideas. From his boyhood on the South Dakota prairie, Alvin Hansen has believed that knowledge can improve the condition of man. In the integrity of that faith he has had the courage never to close his mind and to seek and speak the truth wherever it might lead. But Professor Hansen is to be honored with as much affection as respect. Generation after generation, students have left his seminar and his study not only enlightened but also inspired—inspired with some of his enthusiastic conviction that economics is a science for the service of mankind.

Note

1. The first Alvin Hansen Symposium, in 1995, was titled "Inflation, Unemployment, and Monetary Policy," with principal papers by Robert Solow and John Taylor. The second, in 1998, addressed the question "Should the United States Privatize Social Security?" and featured principal papers by Henry Aaron and John Shoven. The third, in 2002, focused on "Inequality in America," with James Heckman and Alan B. Krueger taking opposing sides on what should be done. The papers and discussions from each of these prior symposia have also been published by the MIT Press.

Offshoring of American Jobs

1   Don't Cry for Free Trade

Jagdish Bhagwati

Turn to the leading American newspapers these days and you will read about the "loss of nerve," even "loss of faith," in free trade by economists. Then, you get incessant protectionist pronouncements from the New Democrats (i.e., those successful in the latest elections) in Congress, and calculated ambiguities on free trade from the Old Democrats (such as Hillary Clinton who infamously asked for a "pause" in ratifying trade deals) as they run for president. When challenged by the proponents of free trade, these politicians now typically say: "Ah, but economists no longer have a consensus on free trade," citing these very same stories they read in the newspapers.

You might think therefore that the days of free trade are behind us in the United States. Indeed, this clamor against free trade is so intense that we may soon turn to PBS and find a *Requiem for Free Trade* composed and performed from England by Sir Paul McCartney. Yet, all this hype reminds me of the cartoon where two dervishes are idly sitting on the desert sands, next to their camels, and one is reading the excitable Cairo newspaper *Al-Ahram* and telling the other: "It says that we are in ferment again."

The truth of the matter is that free trade is alive and well among economists, their analytical arguments in favor of it, developed with great sophistication in the postwar theory of commercial policy, having hardly been dented by any original arguments by the few economists, including Alan Blinder in today's debate, arrayed against it.

The Latest Celebration of the Flight from Free Trade by Economists

If one looks at the most recent flood of journalistic stories on free trade, it is astonishing (as I document in what follows) how often they have been written in funereal over-tones in recent years and with disregard for the historical reality that such stories have been written recurrently in the last twenty years in major newspapers and magazines. The latest stories are by reputed journalists such as Lou Uchitelle of the *New York Times* (January 30, 2007) and the team of Bob Davis and David Wessel in the *Wall Street Journal* (March 28, 2007). They often also profile the "dissenting" economists such as William Baumol (with his coauthor, the hugely reno-wned mathematician Ralph Gomory) and Alan S. Blinder who is before us today.

But if their enthusiasm in imagining the failing health, even the demise, of free trade betrays ignorance of earlier such analyses that came to naught, it is equally noteworthy that these journalists are contradicted by others whose ana-lysis of the robustness of trade among economists is more accurate. Thus, even as Davis and Wessel were writing their story of "second thoughts" on free trade (March 28, 2007) in the *Wall Street Journal*, a conservative newspaper, and pro-claiming that "in many ways, the debate over free trade is moving in . . . the direction [of the skeptics and opponents]," in a telephone interview I drew the attention of Davis to the column by the brilliant and acute Eric Alterman in *The Nation* (February 12, 2007), today's most influential left-wing magazine, which correctly complained instead of the continuing approbation of free trade by economists: "This column is not going to settle the dispute over whether the United States needs a tougher trade policy. I happen to think so, but I don't expect to convince, say, Paul Krugman or Jagdish Bhagwati that I am right and they are wrong. My question is: Why does the opinion of the [political] majority of the country get nothing but contempt in public discourse?"

To gain necessary perspective on the current media stories about the economists' yet-again disappearing consensus on free trade, let me now turn to document different episodes in recent years when false notes of alarm were sounded over free trade, similar in hype to those of the motley crew that I have just cited as the latest journalists writing in a similar vein. I will assess and dismiss the "heretical" arguments that were advanced against free trade in each episode; in fact, I was cast by the media in the role of the defender of free trade in all these episodes.

Earlier Episodes of Media Frenzy

Episode 1: The Rise of Japan: Paul Krugman and Laura Tyson

By far the most striking dissent over free trade, the equivalent of a category 5 storm, came from my MIT student Paul Krugman, one of the truly profound figures today in the theory of international trade, who extended the theory of imperfect competition to trade theory and began to argue that "Free Trade Was Passé After All" in the late 1980s, about two decades ago. The effect on the media, and on the opponents of free trade, was electric, largely because the rise of Japan, and the allegations that it was protectionist while the United States was a free trader, had fed the frenzy that called for a reputable economist as an icon for protectionists.

Robert Kuttner, now the editor of *The American Prospect* and long a skeptic on free trade, celebrated Krugman's apparent heresy. Karen Pennar wrote in *Businessweek* (February 27, 1989), under the heading "The Gospel of Free Trade is Losing Its Apostles," that "Free Trade is good for you . . . Now more and more economists aren't so sure." Aside from Krugman, Laura Tyson (also one of my most distinguished MIT students) was quoted in support of "using trade policies to promote and protect industries and technologies that we believe to be important to our well-being," a position that was rejected by the Stanford economist Michael Boskin in these famous and politically costly words: there is no difference between potato chips and semiconductor chips.

Take just two of the main arguments, starting with Tyson's advocacy of trade policy as an instrument of industrial policy. Tyson claimed that industries with externalities ought to be protected. But the problem with this is that it is very hard for policymakers, and very easy for lobbyists, to decide which industries have the externalities. As the Nobel Laureate Robert Solow, as good a Democrat as you can find, once remarked, I know there are lots of industries where there are four dollars' worth of social output to one dollar's worth of private output; my problem is that I do not know which ones they are. Besides, Michael Schrage of the *Los Angeles Times* decided to actually look at how potato and semiconductor chips were made and, while the proponents of industrial policy obviously thought that semiconductor chips were made with sophisticated technology but potato chips were not, the reality turned out to be very different. Pringle chips, available in mini-bars in fancy hotels, are made by PepsiCo's Frito-Lay subsidiary in virtually auto-mated factories, whereas semiconductors involve mindless fitting of boards by workers with little advanced skills but much patience and ability to survive boredom. Moreover, I noted at the time in a review in the *New Republic* (May 31, 1993) of Laura Tyson's influential book *Who's Bashing Whom?* the exaggerated concern with what you produce as defining your economic destiny is a quasi-Marxist obsession border-ing on folly. You can produce potato chips, export them, and import computers that you may use to do creative things. Equally, you could produce semiconductors, export them, and import potato chips that you could munch as a couch potato, mindlessly watching television and turning into a moron. What you "consume," in a broad sense, is likely to be far more important to you and to your society's well-being than what you produce.

However, Krugman's theoretical modeling of imperfect competition among firms producing differentiated products, and the modeling of oligopolistic industries (by Krugman's contemporaries such as Gene Grossman of Princeton University, my equally remarkable MIT student just after Krugman), did raise problems for free trade at a deeper level.[1] To understand this, consider that the last two centu-ries since Adam Smith wrote about the virtues of free trade had in fact witnessed repeated dissent from front-rank econ-omists such as John Maynard Keynes at the time of the Great Depression. In essence, the argument for free trade is an extension of the argument for the Invisible Hand: if market prices do not reflect social costs, then the Invisible Hand, which uses market prices to guide allocation, will point in the wrong direction. During the Depression, evidently the market wages (which were positive) exceeded the social cost (which was zero because of widespread unemployment). So Keynes became a protectionist. Similarly, if polluters are able to pollute without having to pay for it, we would be over-producing in the polluting industry because its private cost would be below the social cost (which should include the cost being imposed through pollution). Again, the case for free trade would be compromised. Each generation seems to have discovered some market failure, appropriate to its time, which would then undermine the case for free trade.

But, writing in 1963 in the *Journal of Political Economy*, I made a simple point that turned out to be revolutionary for the case for free trade: I argued that if the specific market failure was eliminated by a suitable policy, then the case for free trade would be restored. So, if we were to introduce a "polluter pay" principle (or, tradable permits that would equally charge those who wanted to pollute), we would then be able to fully exploit the gains from trade by adopting free trade. The case for free trade had been restored after two centuries of recurrent doubts.

But there was just one important catch. If the market failure was in domestic "markets" such as labor markets where there may be imperfections such as rural-urban wage differentials or sticky wages that led to wages that exceeded "true" labor cost, then my argument was correct: the vast majority of such imperfections were indeed in domestic markets. But if these imperfections arose in international trade, then fixing these failures would involve using tariffs and so free trade could not be restored as the appropriate policy. So, if a country or its producers had some power in international markets to raise the prices at which they could sell by offering lower quantities for sale, they would do better with what economists call "an optimal tariff," an argument going back to the time of Adam Smith. Krugman was dealing with precisely such imperfections.

But eventually Krugman and other trade economists came back to free trade in several writings, abandoning Kuttner and others to twist in the wind. Essentially, this was done through less watertight, but nonetheless compelling, "political-economy" arguments. One set of economists, among them Avinash Dixit of Princeton University, returned to the fold by saying that "there was no beef": namely, that the product market imperfections were, on empirical investigation, not substantial enough to warrant departing from free trade. Another set of economists, Krugman among them, bought into the argument that protection would make matters worse, not better. My radical Cambridge University teacher Joan Robinson used to say that the Invisible Hand worked by strangulation; the less drastic Krugmanesque demonstration that it was feeble when there were product market imperfections was now combined with the view that the Visible Hand would be crippled instead. Yet others thought that, once we allowed for tariff retaliation, it was unlikely that those who initiated protectionism would survive such retaliation to break open a bottle of champagne.

The protectionists who had celebrated Krugman as their icon were disappointed, even furious: for instance, Kuttner would write fierce critiques of Krugman for years. But the truth of the matter is that, even as these economists came back to the fold on free trade, Japan ceased to be a threat and the hysteria over Japan, thick as a dense fog, subsided. Free trade as our choice policy option was back in business.

Episode 2: The Rise of India and China: Paul Samuelson
But then the rise of India and China would lead to another
category 5 storm. This time, it came from the Nobel Laureate
Paul Samuelson, my teacher at MIT. Writing in the *Journal
of Economic Perspectives* (Summer 2004), he argued, combin-
ing mathematics not accessible to journalists with colorful
language that was, that the advocates of globalization were
ignoring the reality that the rise of India and China would
mean that the welfare of the United States could take a
hit.[2]

Although Samuelson had been careful to stress that this
did not mean that United States should respond with protection, the protectionists thought they had another icon—
this time along with Keynes arguably the greatest economist
of the twentieth century and a longtime proponent of free
trade—in their camp! Kuttner was back in business; soon
there were numerous stories in magazines and newspapers,
similar to those when Krugman had arrived on the scene
almost twenty years earlier: for example, Aaron Bernstein,
"Shaking Up Trade Theory" in *Businessweek* (December 6,
2004), and Steve Lohr, "An Elder Challenges Outsourcing's
Orthodoxy" in the *New York Times* (September 9, 2004),
among many others. Samuelson was careful, as reported by
Steve Lohr in his interview for the *Times* story, to emphasize
that his analysis "was not meant as a justification for protectionist measures." But that was lost in the unwarranted
inferences against free trade by the protectionists.

Now, economists have long appreciated that external
("exogenous") developments could hurt an economy. In
fact, my Cambridge University teacher, Harry Johnson,
wrote exactly on this issue in the 1950s, when the dollar was
scarce and Europeans opted for the pessimistic view that
U.S. growth would harm them (much as many believe to

be the case for the United States as India and China are growing), and he argued that Europe could benefit instead. To see this by analogy, imagine what weather does to your welfare. If a hurricane hits Florida, that hurts. But if a good monsoon arrives in India, that helps.

So, only an unsophisticated economist (and Samuelson is right that there are some, though not necessarily the ones he cited) would rule out the logical possibility that the rise of China and India could harm the United States. That part is not news. But what became news in the popular imagination, fed by much of the media and by protectionists, was that if such a pessimistic possibility actually transpired, the appropriate response was protectionism. To see this again very simply, suppose that a hurricane does damage Florida. If Governor Jeb Bush were to respond to this by shutting off trade with the rest of the United States, if not the world, he would only be increasing Florida's anguish. And Samuelson, whose scholarship is unimpeachable and who is no creature of passions or politics, evidently did not make this elementary error.

As this truth filtered through, as many economists noted this and Samuelson himself emphasized from time to time, the protectionists lost their new icon. Besides, increasingly economists exploring the subject showed that the pessimistic possibility that the rise of India and China to become "more like us" could reduce the U.S. gains from trade by depressing the prices of U.S. exports was not a likely outcome. As countries got similar in endowments, they could profit hugely from trade in similar products (or variety), as another student of mine, Robert Feenstra (who is today the leading applied economist on trade and heads the NBER Program on trade policy) in his Bernhard Harms Prize acceptance speech, and my brilliant Columbia University colleague David Weinstein, demonstrated empirically for the postwar period when Europe and Japan rose again from the ashes. Besides, the immediate political source of worry, the scare created by the outsourcing of a few call-answer and back-office jobs to India (which Alan S. Blinder has bought into, I am afraid), also subsided as it became evident that the notion that all online trade was one-way was at variance with the facts.

Episode 3: India and China and Fear of Outsourcing: Alan S. Blinder

But outsourcing happened to revive again, a couple of years ago, when the distinguished macroeconomist Alan S. Blinder, with us today, who was deeply influenced by Thomas Friedman's bestselling book on globalization— which seemed to translate the credible statement by Bangalore's remarkable IT entrepreneurs-cum-scientists such as Nandan Nilekani that they could do everything that Americans could do into the frightening non sequitur that therefore Indians would do everything that the Americans were doing—published an essay in *Foreign Affairs* (April 2006) that bought into the line that outsourcing of services on the wire would increasingly export American jobs to these countries and presumably imperil the United States and its working and middle classes. So, he was now turned into a new icon for the protectionists even though Blinder always said that he was still a free trader. In fact, Davis and Wessel (*Wall Street Journal*) built their story against free trade around him; he made it to National Public Radio and even to the iconic TV program *Charlie Rose*.

But Blinder seemed to be unaware that outsourcing on the wire (i.e., without the provider and the user having to be in physical proximity as with haircuts), which is mode 1 of supplying services in the General Agreement on Trade in Services (GATS) in the Uruguay Round agreement in 1995, was precisely the mode that the United States and other rich countries were keenest about: they saw that they would be, not losers but, the big winners, as no doubt they are. For all the call-answer services and other low-skill services now imported from countries such as India, there are many more high-skill and high-value services by rich-country professionals in architecture, law, medicine, accounting, and other professions.

But Blinder has now shifted to arguing instead that, as services became tradable online, the number of jobs that would become "vulnerable" would rise pari passu. And he lists upward of forty million jobs today that are so afflicted. He concludes that we need to augment adjustment assistance and improve education in response. There is much that may be said on this as well. For example, if you wish to talk about flux, talking only about mode 1 (online transmission of services) is incomplete. Trade economists know that this is only one of alternative modes in the supply of services: in particular, transmission of services can occur with or without the physical proximity of suppliers and users of the services. Transmitting X-rays digitally from Indiana to be read in India is one example. But then doctors can go to patients, and patients to doctors. The GATS agreement recognizes four distinct modes of service "transactions." As it happens, the different modes were distinguished in a couple of articles in *The World Economy* in the mid-1980s by me and by Gary Sampson and Richard Snape and astonishingly made their way into the GATS agreement within a decade: a remarkable triumph for us economists.[3] I described the basic distinction between service transactions that required physical proximity and those that did not, whereas

Sampson and Snape brilliantly subdivided the former into those where the provider went to the user and the other way around.

Blinder, who does not appear to have known all this when he wrote his celebrated *Foreign Affairs* article,[4] any more than I know about the relevant intricacies of macro-economics where he holds the comparative advantage instead, understates the potential for flux by thinking only of mode 1. In fact, the possible flux arises in more ways today than he talks about. That is also true because of direct foreign investment. For instance, when Senator John Kerry talked about outsourcing, he meant also, confusingly, the phenomenon where a CEO closes down a factory in Nantucket and opens it up in Nairobi, or when that same CEO simply invests in production in Nairobi instead of in Nantucket.

But the bottom line from the viewpoint of trade policy is that hardly any serious trade economist or policymaker has objected to providing adjustment assistance (or improving education) in living memory. The first Adjustment Assistance program in the United States goes back to 1962 during the Kennedy Round negotiations: Kennedy and George Meany of the AFL-CIO signed off on it. Virtually every trade legislation since has tried to improve on it. And many trade economists including myself in the 1970s—and others such as Lael Brainard, Robert Lawrence, and Robert Litan at Brookings in recent years—have written extensively and continually on the subject. Blinder, who started talking poetry ("we are in peril"), has therefore wound up talking prose ("we need adjustment assistance"). We free traders have no problem with him as he is on the same escalator even if he is behind us. If he is to remain the new icon for those who oppose free trade, they have to be pretty desperate.

So, these three balloons with journalists aboard, waving banners against free trade, have lost their helium. Free trade has continued to maintain its credibility among economists. Of course, there have been other, less influential assaults on free trade—among them, I must count that by Baumol and Gomory who have enjoyed nonetheless some exposure, especially from the influential left-wing columnist William Greider in *The Nation* (April 30, 2007) and ironically also from the supply-side economist Paul Craig Roberts in his assault on outsourcing in the *Wall Street Journal*.[5]

I might say simply that Baumol and Gomory make one important but familiar point, with little policy relevance as I argue now. It is the old one, which I learned as a student from R. C. O. Matthews, my Cambridge University tutor in 1954–1956, who had written a classic paper on increasing returns, and with others such as the Nobel Laureate James Meade and Harry Johnson following soon after, who showed that sufficiently increasing returns would imply multiple equilibria and that this in turn implied (among other things) that there could exist a better free-trade equilibrium than the one we may be in. Matthews and Meade, and many others such as Murray Kemp, had made this observation but by using the analytical device that the increasing returns were external to the firm but internal to the industry, a device that enabled perfect competition to be maintained. By the time Krugman was writing his dissertation in the 1970s, economists had learned how to handle imperfect competition, and so Krugman managed brilliantly to show multiple equilibria in this different, and more realistic, setting. Trade economists had known these arguments for almost half a century and taught them from standard textbooks such as mine (with Panagariya and Srinivasan). The analytical buzz therefore from Baumol and Gomory's book was muted.

But when translated into policy prescription, all it could mean was that industrial policy, buttressed Tyson-style by appropriately tailored trade policy, could nudge us toward the "better" equilibrium. But neither author managed to do this, as far as we know. So, paraphrasing Robert Solow on externalities, one might say: yes, if scale economies are important, there could be multiple equilibria and we could use trade and industrial policies to choose a "better" equilibrium; but, alas, who can plausibly compute this better equilibrium? Besides, it is hard to imagine today that, with world markets so large due to the death of distance and extensive postwar trade liberalization, there are any industries or products left where the scale economies do not pale into modest proportions. Baumol and Gomory, a brilliant pair indeed, therefore do not carry any policy salience, in my view.[6]

But one assault that is ongoing, and has had an impact on the New Democrats for sure, is that by economists associated with the AFL-CIO (such as Thea Lee), and with the labor-movement-influenced think tank Economic Policy Institute (such as Lawrence Mishel). In their view the pressure on unskilled wages, and progressively on the middle class as well, is to be traced to trade with poor countries. None of this seems to face up well to the empirical studies of the subject. In an op-ed titled "Technology, not Globalisation, Is Driving Wages Down" in the *Financial Times* (January 4, 2007), I argued that the vast numbers of empirical studies (including those by Krugman) had shown that trade with poor countries had a negligible impact on our workers' absolute real wages (as against the relative wages of the skilled and the unskilled).[7] Nor did alternative ways of tying the depressed wages to trade (and even unskilled, illegal immigration) have any empirical salience. Harvard

University Kennedy School of Government's prolific trade expert Robert Lawrence, in a splendid unpublished recent paper, concurs with this view, concluding that the impact of trade on the slow growth of wages does not "show up" in his analysis of the data.

The New Democrats who continue to believe nonetheless in this imaginary downside of free trade are not doing anyone any good. In fact, they use these erroneous beliefs to stop trade liberalization and to intimidate weak nations into accepting inappropriate labor standards in the hope of raising their cost of production to moderate the force of competition that they fear.[8]

Paul Krugman, in one of his columns in the *New York Times* (May 14, 2007) did say that his own research earlier had argued that trade did not depress wages. But then he added: "But that *may* have changed" (italics added). The suggested reason was that "we're buying a lot more from third-world countries today than we did a dozen years ago." But it is easy to show that you can multiply such imports and still not have any effect on real wages. This particular case against free trade remains unproven and will not rise above the level of innuendos until some dramatic empirical study demonstrates otherwise.[9]

Notes

September 20, 2007. An op-ed based on this article was published in *The Financial Times* on October 10, 2007. Revised slightly on August 19, 2008.

Jagdish Bhagwati is University Professor, Economics and Law, Columbia University, and Senior Fellow at the Council on Foreign Relations. A new edition of his 2004 book, *In Defense of Globalization* (New York: Oxford University Press), has just been released. His latest book on trade, *Termites in the Trading System: How Preferential Trade Agreements Are Undermining Multilateral Free Trade*, was published by Oxford University Press in 2008.

Alan S. Blinder focuses on online outsourcing of services in his own writings as well as in this debate organized by Benjamin M. Friedman; but the issues raised are far more general for free trade itself, and have been advertised as such by the media. So, for both analytical and public-policy reasons, I cast my own contribution very wide, putting Blinder's arguments into necessary perspective. I must also say that I have addressed the economics of the important contributions of Paul Krugman and Paul Samuelson, whom I deal with in addition to Blinder in this essay, in several places and do not repeat them here since my writings are readily available and some are even cited here.

1. I have dealt with the analytics and also the policy implications of Paul Krugman's famous article, "Is Free Trade Passé?," *Journal of Economic Perspectives* 1, no. 2 (Fall 1987): 131–144; and my response in the Bernhard Prize Lecture, "Is Free Trade Passé After All," *Weltwirtschaftliches Archiv*, reprinted as chapter 1 in my *Political Economy and International Economics*, ed. Douglas Irwin (Cambridge, MA: MIT Press, 1991). For the latest, and most easily accessible, post-Krugman statement of the postwar theory of commercial policy, see chapter 1 of my *Free Trade Today* (Princeton, NJ: Princeton University Press, 2002).

2. Paul Samuelson, "Where Ricardo and Mill Rebut and Confirm Arguments of Mainstream Economists Supporting Globalization," *Journal of Economic Perspectives* 18, no. 3 (Summer 2004): 135–146.

My own article, "The Muddles over Outsourcing," written with Arvind Panagariya and T. N. Srinivasan, appeared in the same journal (*Journal of Economic Perspectives* 18, no. 4 [Fall 2004]: 93–114), right after Samuelson's, and was regarded by many in the media as a "response" to Samuelson. It was not; we were not even aware of Samuelson's article when we wrote ours. Our article was in fact the first analytical exercise, with a number of theoretical models, exploring trade in services; and it was also the first to argue that several critics and commentators, including economists, were muddling up very different notions of what "outsourcing" meant and hence muddling their arguments, in turn.

3. Jagdish Bhagwati, "Splintering and Disembodiment of Services in Developing Nations," *The World Economy* 7 (June 1984): 133–143; and Gary P. Sampson and Richard H. Snape, "Identifying the Issues in Trade in Services," *The World Economy* 8 (June 1985): 171–181.

4. A referee objected that Blinder is aware of the GATS and of the different modes of service transactions. I am sure that this is true now. However, my reseach associate has searched Blinder's *Foreign Affairs* article and found no mention of GATS or of the different modes.

5. William Baumol and Ralph Gomory, *Global Trade and Conflicting National Interests* (Cambridge, MA: MIT Press, 2000).

6. There is one other argument in Baumol and Gomory that does not rely on scale economies. It is simply that technology may diffuse abroad and that this may create difficulties for the United States. This is similar to the concerns that India and China may become more like the United States in terms of their endowments and hence the gains from trade may diminish for the United States. But I have dealt with that argument already in discussing Samuelson.

7. There has also been dispute about how stagnant real wages have been, with some economists such as Marvin Kosters and Richard Cooper arguing that, once benefits and perks outside of strict wages are allowed for, the stagnation turns into slow growth. But I avoid this debate, arguing only about the explanation of stagnation or slow growth, as the case may be.

8. I have dealt with the phenomenon of export protectionism in the form of demands for higher labor standards in the poor countries in my book, *In Defense of Globalization* (New York: Oxford University Press, 2004), and particularly in the afterword to the new edition issued in August 2007. In discussing the protectionism that now characterizes the New Democrats, I have dealt with this issue in several other places, such as the *Financial Times*, and do not enter that set of arguments here.

9. As it happens, Robert Lawrence's recent empirical research shows that Krugman's "may have" needs to be replaced by "has not."

2   Offshoring: Big Deal, or Business as Usual?

Alan S. Blinder

President Bush is on an eight-day tour of Asia. He's visiting American jobs.

—David Letterman in 2006

More things are tradable than were tradable in the past, and that's a good thing.

—Greg Mankiw in 2004

Economists set themselves too easy, too useless a task if in tempestuous seasons they can only tell us that when the storm is long past the ocean is flat again.

—John Maynard Keynes in 1923

If there is a live intellectual debate over offshoring—which is, after all, the premise of this symposium—what is it all about? What separates those of us who worry about the effects of offshoring on the U.S. labor market from those who, like Greg Mankiw in 2004 and Jagdish Bhagwati today, see offshoring of services as just the latest expansion of international trade and, therefore, as "a good thing" for the United States—period?[1]

A Definition

Perhaps I should start with a definition because "offshoring" is often confused with "outsourcing," which is different. Specifically, a job is *outsourced* when it is contracted *out of the company*—presumably to another company. The *country* in which the job is now being done is irrelevant. So, for example, Citibank can outsource the back-office operations of its U.S. credit card business to a company in South Dakota or to one in South Korea. In the latter case, the jobs are also offshored; in the former case, they are not.

Offshoring, by contrast, means moving jobs *out of the country*, whether or not they leave the company. Thus, Microsoft offshores (but does not outsource) jobs when it moves jobs from its software laboratory in Redmond, Washington, to its laboratory in Cambridge, England. But if Microsoft hires another company to provide software lab services in the United States, those jobs are outsourced but not offshored. And, of course, if Microsoft contracts with Infosys to get the work done in Bangalore, the jobs are both outsourced and offshored. The National Academy of Public Administration (2006, 42) suggests defining offshoring as "U.S. firms shifting service and manufacturing activities abroad to unaffiliated firms or their own affiliates." That seems a workable definition to me.

The offshoring phenomenon, which is about the *location of work*, does not correspond neatly to any category of standard international trade data. Much U.S. service offshoring today counts as imports of services. But many U.S. service imports—for example, tourist services consumed abroad—do not constitute offshoring because the people who do the work (in hotels, restaurants, etc.) deliver their services locally. Furthermore, some offshoring is classified as foreign direct investment (FDI), rather than as trade—Microsoft's building of a lab in England being a prime example.

Finally, I come to the most slippery part of the concept—the one that is nearly impossible to measure. In line with the preceding definition, we would like to say that a U.S. company offshores jobs when it creates *new* jobs to serve our market, but locates them overseas. So, for example, if a U.S. manufacturer expands production by opening a factory in China for export back to the United States, we want to say that the jobs in that factory have been offshored—even though they never existed in the United States. Measuring this particular type of offshoring requires answering counterfactual questions—like "Would those jobs otherwise have been created in the United States?"—that will never be captured in official data.

The Debate

With the definition now (hopefully) clear, let me turn next to what the debate is *not* about. First, it definitely is not about the validity of the theory of comparative advantage. David Ricardo got that approximately right about two centuries ago, and I have little or nothing to add. Besides, I am not so foolish as to engage in a debate over the nuances of trade theory with one of the finest trade theorists of our age. Let me just state—as clearly and unequivocally as I can—that I am *not* claiming that the United States is about to lose comparative advantage in everything! (Don't laugh; I have actually been accused of that.)

Second, the debate is not even about the common presumption that every nation gains from trade, although that particular "theorem" does require an important footnote that I will mention shortly.

Third, it is not about the comparative statics of how either social welfare or employment compares in one equilibrium state (say, after offshoring) versus another (say, before offshoring). I am willing to stipulate that, when all the dust has settled, the U.S. economy as a whole, though certainly not every American, is likely to be better off because of service offshoring. In particular, we worry-warts are not concerned that the U.S. faces a bleak future of mass secular unemployment. Thus I am happy to accept Bhagwati, Panagariya, and Srinivasan's (2004, 94) assessment that offshoring "is fundamentally just a trade phenomenon; that is, subject to the usual theoretical *caveats* and practical responses, [it] leads to gains from trade, and its effects on jobs and wages are not qualitatively different from those of conventional trade in goods." We will not argue about that.

What, then, *is* the offshoring debate about? Leaving aside the lunatic fringes (each side can name its own favorite lunatics), I believe it is about whether the offshoring of service jobs from rich countries like the United States to poor ones like India is likely to be a *big deal*, something I have compared to a new industrial revolution (Blinder 2006a), or simply more *business as usual*—yet another routine expansion of international trade, as Bhagwati, Panagariya, and Srinivasan (2004) say. Count me as firmly in the first camp. What makes me a worrywart is the belief that the confluence of rapid improvements in information and communications technology (ICT) coupled with the entry of giants like China and India into the global economy is creating a situation that, while perhaps not theoretically novel, may be historically unprecedented. When I say it will be a "big deal," I mean that offshoring will force major changes in the U.S. industrial structure, in what Americans do to earn their livings, probably in wages, almost certainly in job security and turnover, and so on. As I noted in my 2006 essay in *Foreign Affairs* (Blinder 2006a, 113), "Sometimes a quantitative change is so large that it brings about qualitative changes." I suspect service offshoring will be like that.

In thinking through the consequences of the confluence of ICT breakthroughs and vast new pools of labor, it is crucial to keep in mind a distinction I emphasized in Blinder 2006a—the difference between *personally delivered services* and *impersonally delivered services*. Impersonal services are the ones that can be delivered electronically from afar with little or no degradation of quality—either now or sometime in the future when the technology has improved (e.g., keyboard data entry, manuscript editing, etc.). They are therefore either actually or prospectively *tradable* and thus potentially offshorable. Personal services, by contrast, are the ones that either cannot be delivered electronically (e.g., child care) or that suffer severe degradation of quality when so delivered (e.g., surgery). They are therefore, for all practical purposes, nontradable.[2]

We may be standing, right now, at a historical cusp. Looking *backward*, the crucial labor market divide has been the familiar one: between jobs that require high levels of education and jobs that do not. Roughly speaking, highly educated workers have fared far better than poorly educated ones for a generation. But looking *forward*, the more critical distinction may be the unconventional divide between personal and impersonal service jobs. And the interesting thing is that *these two divisions of the workforce are almost completely unrelated*. A few examples will illustrate what I mean.

It seems to me unlikely that the services of either taxi drivers or brain surgeons will ever be delivered electronically by long distance. The first is a "bad job" with negligible educational requirements; the second is just the reverse. On the other hand, typing services (a low-skill job) and security analysis (a high-skill job) are already being delivered electronically from India—albeit on a small scale so far. Most physicians need not fear that their jobs will be moved offshore, but perhaps radiologists should.[3] The work of policemen will not be replaced by electronic delivery, but the work of security guards who monitor sites by television might be. I could go on and on with examples like these.

Briefly stated—and this is something to which I will return—the reasons why I see service offshoring as a large and potentially disruptive force for the United States (and for other rich countries) are that (a) so many Americans now earn their living providing services,[4] (b) the range of services that can be delivered electronically is sure to expand as the technology improves, and (c) the number of Indian, Chinese, and other workers who are capable of providing those services will only grow over time—perhaps explosively. Does anyone disagree with any of those three propositions?

That said, no one can predict the future. So why bother to debate *now* whether service offshoring will *eventually* turn out to be business as usual or a big deal? Why not just wait and see? My answer is simple: the answer matters for public policy. If this new wave of international trade constitutes no more than business as usual, then the appropriate policy response is approximately nothing. With only minor assists, laissez-faire will fare just fine; the main trick is to avoid protectionism. But if offshoring will eventually amount to something approaching a new industrial revolution, then a variety of policy responses may be called for.

I will return to policy responses at the end. First let me frame the intellectual debate—just to establish that we worrywarts are not all muddled thinkers.[5]

Some Self-Evident Truths

Since Adam Smith and Thomas Jefferson published their best work at exactly the same time, let me begin the debate by holding a few truths to be self-evident.

First, as just mentioned, we worriers do not question either the validity or the importance of the theory of comparative advantage. Nor do we doubt the advisability of exploiting a country's comparative advantages rather than flailing out against those of other countries. I yield to no one in my defense of free trade.[6] And nothing said herein should be construed as favoring protectionism in any way.

Second, I understand that trade is a two-way street. The eventual post-offshoring equilibrium *cannot* have the United States producing *only* nontradables and exporting *nothing*. Precisely what we will export then is a good question, for our trade patterns may have to change substantially. (More on that later.) And we need not have balanced trade in goods and services because the United States will surely continue to export financial assets for a long time. But America must and will remain a great exporting nation as well as a great importing nation. After all, market-driven trade patterns depend on *comparative* advantages, not *absolute* advantages.

Third, comparative advantage in the modern world has relatively little to do with natural resource endowments. David Ricardo understood well why Portugal, not England, grew the grapes. These are basically the same reasons why, even today, Brazil exports bananas and Saudi Arabia exports oil. But for most of modern trade, we can mostly ignore natural endowments. Silicon Valley did not become what it is today because of a natural abundance of silicon. Nor did the United States develop a strong comparative advantage in aircraft because our air provides more lift.

When it comes to trade in services (and much else), the skills of a country's workforce matter much more than its climate, soil, or natural resources. It follows from this obvious insight that, in an important sense, comparative advantage is made not born. A determined and successful country can *create* comparative advantage for itself in industries and/or tasks where it formerly had none—as, for example, Japan did so brilliantly in automobiles and electronics. Thus, as Bhagwati (1997) has aptly put it, modern comparative advantage (as opposed to resource-based comparative advantage) may be "kaleidoscopic," meaning that it can move around from one country to another in response to changes in costs.

Fourth, I come to the footnote mentioned earlier. Trade theorists have long understood that it is theoretically possible for a country to end up worse off when a "new entrant" country comes along and takes away its comparative advantage in one or more important industries.[7] Indeed, comparative advantage does not have to be *lost*. As Hymans and Stafford (1995) show, the home country can become worse off if the foreign country merely gets *better* at producing the good that is (and remains) the home country's comparative advantage.

In the offshoring context, think about India either taking away or shrinking the United States' former comparative advantages in a number of service occupations.[8] Of course, even if lost or fading comparative advantage is the problem, protectionism is not the solution. In fact, it will probably only inflict further damage—which takes us back to my first self-evident truth. However, loss of comparative advantage in major industries and occupations is a serious cause for concern *in the future*. And we worrywarts are worried about it.

Fifth, and finally, it cannot be emphasized enough that the debate about the "threat" from offshoring is not about the nature of the eventual equilibrium position. For example, we big-dealers do not believe that the offshoring of millions of service jobs will lead to mass unemployment in the United States. However, we do foresee a massive *transition* as millions of workers are rudely reallocated by the market mechanism.

Unfortunately, the vast majority of trade theory pertains to the analysis of full-employment equilibrium states and has little or nothing to say about either unemployment or transitions.[9] Too often, economists simply label certain things "transition costs" and then proceed to ignore them. But when it comes to a phenomenon as big as service offshoring, such a cavalier treatment strikes me as more than a trifle hypermetropic.[10] In addition to job losses, it is quite likely that, by stripping away their previous immunity to foreign competition, offshoring will depress the real wages of many service workers in the United States who do *not* lose their jobs.

Now, About That Transition . . .

So both my intellectual focus and my practical concerns center on the transition, not on the ultimate equilibrium state. Let us therefore pose, and attempt to answer, a series of questions, both qualitative and quantitative, about the likely nature of this transition. Here, the "truths" become less than self-evident because we are speculating about the future.

I start with the hypothesis that offshoring will usher in a massive and disruptive transition—a new industrial revolution, if you will. Past industrial revolutions have changed the faces of societies, causing great dislocation before, ultimately, leaving those societies much better off. I expect this one to follow that same pattern. But before we reach the promised land, I suspect that we Americans will experience a nasty transition, lasting for decades, in which not just millions but tens of millions of jobs are lost to off-shoring. (That's gross, not net, losses, of course.) Which brings to mind the quotation from Keynes at the start of this chapter. I want us to think about the tempestuous season, not just the eventually flat ocean.

Some economists object to this worry about the transition by noting that the transfer of more than 20 percent of American labor from manufacturing to other sectors from the 1960s to now was accomplished rather smoothly. So why worry about the transition out of impersonal service jobs? But I, for one, am not convinced that the transition from manufacturing to services (which is still going on) has been that smooth. Millions of individuals and hundreds of communities paid substantial costs—almost always without compensation—so that the rest of us could reap the benefits. Some displaced manufacturing workers never regained their previous economic status. Even today, with manufacturing down to 10 percent of total U.S. employ-ment, many policymakers are still fixated on maintaining (or even restoring) our manufacturing base. That does not lead to the best policy prescriptions.

A similarly sized transition from impersonal to personal service jobs would mean moving millions of workers to new jobs, which is vastly more service offshoring than has occurred to date. While estimates are fragmentary, it seems a good bet that offshoring to date has cost fewer than a million American *service* jobs.[11] But I suggested in Blinder

2006a that the job losses experienced to date are probably just the tip of a much larger iceberg whose contours will only be revealed in time. Why do I say this?

Since we have no crystal ball, let's do a thought experiment. Start with a stylized multicountry, static equilibrium model of international trade in a wide variety of goods and services. N countries, M goods, and L factors of production (e.g., different types of labor), if you like to talk that way. There is full employment everywhere. (Isn't there always, in trade models?) The N countries vary greatly in their stage of development, the skill mixes of their workforces, and their patterns of comparative advantage and disadvantage. The gains from trade in the M goods are therefore bountiful, and free trade will realize many of them. Now let's perturb this Panglossian equilibrium with two big shocks.

First, add three large but poor nations to the world economy. Of course, I do not mean that three "new" countries literally rise like Atlantis from the sea. Think of them as having been disengaged from the global economy and then joining it in a big way. My empirical counterparts are, of course, China, India, and the former Soviet bloc. These three new countries bring a huge amount of additional labor into the global economy, some of it highly skilled. But they bring in comparatively little new capital. World factor proportions therefore shift substantially against labor. Suppose further that one of these new nations, call it "India," has millions of workers who speak fluent English—the language of the biggest, richest economy, which I will call "the United States." These workers in India are thus able to provide U.S. firms with many services that require facility in English. We might say that, among poor countries, India has a comparative advantage in the electronic delivery of impersonal services *in English*.

What happens in the model? The first thing most economists would think of is a change in relative factor prices,
perhaps a dramatic one. There should be downward pressure on the general level of real wages around the world.
The impact should be especially large on the wages of highly
tradable types of labor in the rich countries, especially where
a lot of specific human capital is involved. Correspondingly,
there should be upward pressure on the returns to capital.
Looking around the world today, that all sounds pretty
realistic; internationally mobile capital has been doing a lot
better than immobile labor lately. As Richard Freeman
(2005, 3) has put it: "The entry of China, India and the
former Soviet bloc to the global capitalist economy is a
turning point in economic history" that will pose "a long
and difficult transition for workers throughout the world."

Now bring in the second shock, which is technological.
Suppose rapid improvements in ICT greatly expand the
range of services that can be traded. One consequence is
that many jobs that were formerly considered nontradable
become at least potentially tradable. (Some examples are
accountants, security analysts, and radiologists.) Comparative advantage is up for grabs in these newly tradable
services—after all, there was no trade in them before. More
than likely, such comparative advantage will be made not
born. And the patterns of trade that emerge are unlikely to
be resource-based to any important extent—unless you
classify workforce skills and speaking English as resources.
Thus, in particular, India may prove to have a strong comparative advantage in a range of newly tradable services
that require English language skills. And the workers who
hold those same jobs in the United States will find that
their jobs are suddenly "in play"—which will put even
more downward pressure on their wages. It is not a pretty

picture for American call center operators or computer programmers.

Now add one more worrisome factor to the mix: the cost disease of the personal services, also known as Baumol's disease.[12] Baumol's disease, you will recall, is the idea that the prices of personal services, in which there is little scope for productivity improvement, are destined to rise relative to the prices of either manufactured goods (Baumol's central example) or impersonal services (my corollary here), which do experience regular productivity gains. It explains, for example, why the relative prices of live performances, college education, mail delivery, and health care services all have risen sharply over the decades.[13]

Ever-rising relative prices have predictable consequences because demand curves slope downward. Specifically, Baumol's disease predicts *decreasing* relative demands for personal services and *increasing* relative demands for goods and impersonal services—unless differential income elasticities overwhelm the relative price effects.[14] Here Baumol's disease connects to the offshoring problem in a rather disconcerting way. I have argued that changing trade patterns will keep almost all *personal* service jobs at home while a large number of jobs producing goods and *impersonal* services will migrate overseas. When you add to that the likelihood that demands for many of these costly personal services may shrink relative to the demands for ever-cheaper manufactured goods and impersonal services, you realize that the rich countries may have some major readjustments ahead of them.

But, of course, all is not negative. The entry of the three large-but-poor countries into the global economy broadens markets and creates expanded opportunities not only for U.S. capital, but also for certain types of U.S. labor—including some *service* labor. The United States will be "onshoring" jobs as well as offshoring them. So, for example, it may be a very good time to be an American investment banker, movie star, lawyer, scientist, etc.—maybe even a college professor.

Furthermore, the cost reductions achieved by the industries that reap large gains from offshoring are analogous to productivity improvements in the United States—which, other things equal, will raise the demands for both labor and capital in those industries.[15] Perhaps most important, these productivity gains will raise U.S. standards of living—which is, after all, the fundamental purpose of trade. These and other favorable adjustments are also part of the transition, a transition we must welcome, not impede.

That said, I can't help believing—and this is what makes me a worrywart rather than a relaxed, business-as-usual guy—that the gross job losses in the rich, English-speaking countries will (a) continue for decades, (b) eventually be huge, (c) pose a variety of difficult adjustment problems, and (d) dominate the political economy landscape for years. Let me take up each of these four claims one at a time, turning as I do so from abstract trade theory to what may become the new practical realities for the United States. Remember, my self-assigned task is not to overturn received trade theory, but only to defend the "big deal" hypothesis.

Will Offshoring Continue for Decades?

Actually, I'd like first to hold one more truth to be self-evident: that the two big, historic forces driving the offshoring phenomenon are going to be with us for some time.

The rate of technological change in ICT may accelerate or decelerate from its recent dizzying pace. I do not know. Nor do I know in which novel directions future developments will take us. But I am confident that ICT will keep on improving inexorably, thereby steadily increasing the range *and complexity* of the services that can be delivered electronically, and the quality of that delivery. Does anyone seriously doubt that network connections, voice recognition systems, the quality of video conferencing, artificial intelligence, and the like will all be much better and cheaper a generation from now than they are today?

Thus I was dumbstruck when one of my critics claimed that my rough estimates of offshorability in Blinder 2006a are far too high because "most jobs at risk of offshoring today or in the near future are likely to be at risk in twenty years, while *jobs not at risk today are likely to not be at risk in the future*" (Atkinson 2006, 3; emphasis added). Read those italicized words again. They remind me of the apocryphal story of the commissioner of the U.S. Patent Office who allegedly urged President McKinley to abolish the office because "everything that can be invented has already been invented." I claim no clairvoyance. But it is a virtual certainty that an increasing array of services will become offshorable over time—that is, many jobs that are *not now* at risk *will be* at risk in the future.

Here's an example I like to use with audiences like this one. Think about a highly skilled, well-paid occupation with which we are all familiar: teaching economics in a university. Now here's my question. Twenty or thirty years from now, will Economics 101 lectures at Princeton University be delivered by a lifelike hologram of a well-educated and well-spoken professor who is actually in Mumbai, but who can see and hear the Princeton students via video and audio hookups—and who earns one-fifth of what I do?[16] Actually, I think the answer to the question for Princeton and Harvard is probably no. Our massive endowments will allow us the

luxury of maintaining the more expensive personal treatment for longer. But what about the 99.9 percent of colleges
and universities that are not as well-endowed and that will
be under unremitting cost pressures from Baumol's disease?
It is at least conceivable to me that this eminently *personal*
service will one day become an *impersonal* service. Every
reader can surely think of other examples. In imagining
what might be possible by 2039, try to remember how much
things have changed since 1979.

The second major driver of offshoring is the emergence of
India, China, and other countries. It seems a good bet that
these countries will continue to provide not just large but
increasing numbers of skilled workers to the world economy
for at least a generation. It takes time to train your labor
force, even when your economy is growing at 10 percent
per year. Thus I have no quarrel at all with Bhagwati,
Panagariya, and Srinivasan's (2004, 108) observation: "The
notion that India and China will quickly educate 300 million
of their citizens to acquire [the] sophisticated and complex
skills at stake borders on the ludicrous ... Adding 300
million to the pool of the skilled workers in India and China
will take some decades." Read that last sentence again. Two
to three decades seems to be about the right time frame
for thinking about service offshoring, and three hundred
million is roughly equal to the present workforces of the
United States and Western Europe combined! As I say: it's
a big deal.

Will Offshoring Eventually Be Huge?

How large will the (gross, not net) job losses eventually
be? No one knows, of course. Bhagwati, Panagariya, and
Srinivasan meant to *minimize* the perceived threat to U.S.

workers when they wrote the words just quoted. But most American workers won't find them very reassuring. Of course, only a fraction of those hypothetical three hundred million new workers will compete for what we now think of as American jobs. But even if only, say, one-fifth of them do so, sixty million is more than enough to create something akin to a new industrial revolution.

In a current working paper (Blinder 2008), I make some educated guesses about how many U.S. jobs are or will be *potentially offshorable*.[17] My intent there is to guesstimate the *outer limits* of *potential* offshoring, not the *likely amount* of *actual* offshoring (which is unknowable). Just as there are still steelworkers and textile workers in American manufacturing plants, despite decades of offshoring in these industries, so will there still be American workers doing impersonal service jobs in the United States a generation from now. Here, in a nutshell, is how I made my guesstimate. (And, by the way, I welcome both other estimates and suggestions for improvement.)

I began with the premise that the right way to think about offshorability is to study the characteristics of *jobs* (e.g., do they require personal contact?), not the characteristics of *workers* (e.g., how many years of education to they have?). So I gathered data on the approximately eight hundred occupations in the six-digit Standard Occupational Classification (SOC) of the Bureau of Labor Statistics (BLS). For virtually all of these, the O*NET, an online service developed for the BLS as a replacement for the old Dictionary of Occupational Titles (DOT), offers a wealth of descriptive information about the occupation, including the main work activities that characterize the job. After giving up on using these data to create an *objective* ranking of the eight hundred occupations by their degree of offshorability,[18]

I used O*NET data to create a *subjective* ranking running from one hundred (the most offshorable jobs) to zero (the least offshorable).

In developing those rankings, I leaned heavily on two critical determinants of offshorability. The first has been emphasized already. Can the work be delivered to a remote location—which, for services, generally means electronic transmission? And if so, how severely is the quality degraded? Using information in the job descriptions provided in the O*NET, I rated each occupation on this criteria subjectively. For example, the importance of personal, face-to-face contact with end users was used as a strong negative indicator of offshorability.

The second criterion is even more obvious, and it is at least closer to being objective: Must the job be performed at a specific U.S. location? So, for example, data entry, telemarketing, and computer programming were rated as highly offshorable (index numbers at or near 100), while nursing, judging or arguing cases in court, and working in a day care center were rated as impossible to offshore (index numbers at or near 0). Using these and other criteria, I assigned a number between 0 and 100 to each occupation, indicating its potential offshorability. Those numbers were then used to create the histogram reproduced below as figure 2.1.

From this histogram, deriving an estimate of the number of jobs that are potentially offshorable is a simple matter of counting down from the righthand tail—once you decide where to place the dividing line between jobs that are and are not offshorable.[19] I drew that line in three different places, thereby creating three estimates of the fraction of jobs that are potentially offshorable—which I would characterize as conservative (22.2%), moderate (25.6%), and

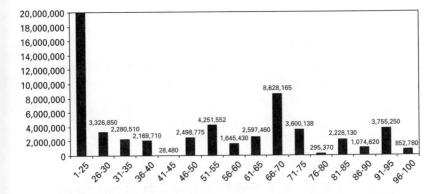

Figure 2.1
Distribution of employment by offshorability index
Source: Blinder 2008.

aggressive (29.0%). Based on today's workforce, that range corresponds to about thirty to forty million jobs—a big number. While the range is wide in absolute size, it is narrow in the relevant policy sense: the policy implications do not hinge on whether the correct number is closer to thirty million or to forty million. Estimates of, say, four million or one hundred million potentially offshorable jobs would have been different.

Major Adjustment Problems?

I am not—repeat, *not*—claiming that thirty to forty million Americans will lose their jobs because of offshoring. Rather, this is my rough estimate of the number of jobs that will face *potential* foreign competition. Only a fraction of them will actually be moved offshore. In addition, this transition will take some time—perhaps decades—and slower transitions are easier to handle than faster ones. Furthermore, there will also be some onshoring, as American businesses export new and expanded services to the rest of the world.

As I suggested earlier, if you compare the original pre-offshoring equilibrium to the eventual post-offshoring equilibrium once the adjustment is complete, a reasonable estimate of the likely *net* job loss is *zero*. But *gross* job losses will be huge, leading to a great deal of churning, much displacement (and reemployment) of labor, and many difficult adjustments—occupational, geographical, and otherwise.

Let's start with employment. Here, my main (and obvious) point was anticipated by Bhagwati (1997, 22), who noted that "the changed external environment of a kaleidoscopic comparative advantage" leads to "increased job insecurity . . . directly by increasing job displacements." Furthermore, he added, this "phenomenon is a definite and enduring change." I agree. Why doesn't Bhagwati vintage 2007 agree with Bhagwati vintage 1997?

To a macroeconomist, it is natural to subdivide the job displacement that offshoring might cause into three components. First, more job churn probably raises the equilibrium or natural rate of unemployment,[20] though perhaps not by very much owing to the huge job churn that is normal for the U.S. labor market. Second, the changes wrought by offshoring will probably lead to substantial "structural" unemployment due to occupational/skill mismatch. And third, there may well be substantial amounts of "Keynesian" unemployment due to deficient demand during the transition years. A brief word on each is in order.[21]

First, frictional unemployment from job churn. When the gross job destruction rate rises, the pool of unemployed workers also rises unless the gross job creation rate rises pari passu. My belief—and only time will tell whether this is correct—is that offshoring per se will lead to far more job destruction than job creation in the United States,[22] and to just the opposite in India and China. If so, the "full employment" unemployment rate will rise. Any good macroeconomist will point out that this rise in the natural rate of unemployment should be transitory—this job churn represents net job loss only in the short run, not in the long run. But the transition period could last for years.

Next comes structural unemployment from mismatch. The heart of my argument is that, over a period of decades, many millions of Americans may find themselves displaced from their previous jobs in impersonal service occupations and forced to find work elsewhere. Open, flexible labor markets do a remarkably good job of handling large-scale reallocations like that. After all, more than four million American workers either lose or gain a job (or both) each month. But the adjustment will be neither painless nor immediate—after all, changing *occupations* is a lot harder than changing *jobs*. In the interim, structural unemployment will rise.

Finally, there is Keynesian unemployment from deficient aggregate demand. Job losses from offshoring arise when the demand for certain services shifts from the United States to other countries. When that happens, U.S. imports rise, shifting the trade balance in the negative direction and reducing aggregate demand. In a Keynesian world—and that, after all, is the world in which we live—deficient demand leads to higher (cyclical) unemployment. Once again, any competent macroeconomist will point out that this extra bit of unemployment is transitory. But most of us feel that the proper time frame for thinking about "transitory" Keynesian unemployment is a year or two, not a month or two.

Now turn from jobs to wages. Even where jobs are simply rendered *offshorable*, rather than actually moved *offshore*, the threat of potential offshoring would be expected to create downward pressure on real wages. Might this be happening already? My priors told me no; wage loss from offshoring is something to worry about in the future, not now. But a simple wage regression for 2004, run using the constructed data on offshorability mentioned earlier, says otherwise. Specifically, in Blinder 2008 I ran the following conventional log wage equation across 291 occupations:[23]

$$\ln(w) = \text{const.} + 0.152ED - 0.138D_{86\text{-}100} - 0.118D_{76\text{-}85} + \text{other dummies}$$
$$\quad\quad\quad\quad\quad (19.1)\quad\quad (2.10)\quad\quad\quad (1.42)$$

where t-ratios are in parentheses, w is the median wage in the occupation, ED is (approximately) average years of education, $D_{86\text{-}100}$ is a dummy variable equal to one for occupations with offshoring scores between 86 and 100 (the most offshorable occupations), $D_{76\text{-}85}$ is a corresponding dummy for occupations with offshoring scores between 76 and 85, and none of the other six offshoring dummies come close to statistical significance.

Taken at face value, this regression says that workers in the most offshorable jobs were already paying an estimated 13 percent wage penalty in 2004, given their educational attainment.[24] This is a surprising—and, to me, provocative—finding. It is hard to imagine that the mere threat of offshoring was having such large effects on wages by 2004. Nevertheless, the empirical fact remains: controlling for education, wages in the most offshorable jobs were unusually low.

Furthermore, the transition costs caused by the adjustment to offshoring will not be limited to those I have just discussed: a "transitory" rise in unemployment (that could last many years) and potentially permanent declines in real wages for workers in highly offshorable occupations. There will also be sizable adjustment costs if tens of millions of American workers must change occupations, move geographically, or do both. Capital, which is not 100 percent malleable, will also have to be redeployed.

A Big Political Issue?

As we all know, free trade is under attack in the United States (and elsewhere) today, even though the unemployment rate has been low until very recently,[25] and offshoring has cost few American jobs to date. We are left to imagine what might happen to public support for free trade if, say, ten million more jobs were offshored, wages were further depressed, and job market churn, mismatch, and Keynesian unemployment combined to raise the unemployment rate.

Protectionism will not be an effective remedy for any of these problems. While goods arriving on ships can perhaps be kept out of the United States by the Coast Guard, electronically delivered services arriving via wireless transmission cannot be. But the fact that protectionism will not work does not mean that it will not be tried. In fact, I fear that large-scale offshoring will seriously undermine public support for the open trading system in the United States and other rich countries. In this context, four things are worth noting.

First, and without repeating arguments I have already made, I believe the adjustment to offshoring will be of major magnitude, will last a long time, and will create millions of losers. Those are precisely the ingredients needed to create a big political issue—even before you throw in the demagoguery.

Second, service offshoring is exposing an entirely new class of people to the joys of competition from cheap foreign labor. Factory workers in rich countries have come to understand, sometimes through bitter experience, that people in emerging-market countries can do their jobs pretty well—and at a fraction of their wages. While these manufacturing workers do not relish foreign competition, they have come to see it as one of the hazards of modern industrial life—like bankruptcies and recessions. But white-collar professionals have not. American computer programmers have already felt the sting of offshoring. But as of now, accountants, lawyers, editors, radiologists, and the like really have not. So this will be a new experience for them, and it is predictable that they will not like it. What's more, these professionals are, on average, better educated, more vocal and articulate, and probably more politically engaged than the blue-collar workers who have been dealing with offshoring for decades. So this new class of trade victims could well prove to be a potent political force. Maintaining free trade in this environment will be a challenge.

Third, both the adjustment costs and the ultimate gains from trade will be larger for the United States and other *English-speaking* countries than for other rich countries that do not speak English because the English speakers can and will make more use of electronically delivered services. India (and, to a lesser extent, the Philippines) will continue to exploit their linguistic comparative advantage by providing the U.S. with a huge pool of skilled and semiskilled service labor that is proficient in English. By contrast, it is impossible to find comparably large pools of potential service workers in poor countries who are proficient in, say, Japanese or

German. So service offshoring probably poses much larger transition problems for the United States than for either continental Europe or Japan.[26]

Fourth, the United States has always done a woefully inadequate job of what economists call "compensating losers." It has been known since the beginning of trade theory that changes in international trade create both winners and losers. The basic gains-from-trade "theorem" is that the gains to the winners exceed the losses to the losers, leaving the nation as a whole ahead.[27] That's nice to know, and it is the main reason why almost all economists support free trade. But trade liberalization is not, repeat *not*, a Pareto improvement unless the losers are actually, not theoretically, compensated—which they almost never are.

For all these reasons, my crystal ball tells me that offshoring may be one of the biggest political issues in economics over the next generation. What, then, can policymakers do to make the transition faster and/or less painful—which might help defuse protectionist sentiment and preserve the liberal trading system? My responses fall into three baskets.

Policy I: Building a Better Safety Net

The first basket picks up on the observation I just made. While we have had one form or another of trade adjustment assistance (TAA) in the United States since the early 1960s, our track record with it is, in a word, miserable. With some exceptions, TAA is not very generous; it has been criticized for providing more assistance than adjustment; and the number of people actually served by TAA programs is pretty small. For example, during fiscal year 2006, the U.S. Department of Labor reported about 53,500 new cases of financial assistance and about 36,000 new cases of job training under TAA.

One reason for these shortcomings is that TAA has never been a high priority for our national government—an attitude that may change as increasing numbers of Americans come to need it. But a second reason is that TAA programs have neither been particularly well-designed nor well-advertised to date.[28] We simply must find ways to provide TAA better than we have in the past. For openers, we need to cover service workers.

That said, it is often difficult to know which displaced workers lose their jobs to trade competition (and therefore qualify for TAA) and which lose their jobs for other reasons. Nor is it always sensible to try to figure it out. Why, for example, should workers displaced by trade be treated better than workers displaced by technology? Posing that question suggests that policymakers should perhaps concentrate on repairing and extending the social safety net for *all* displaced workers. Better unemployment insurance, a more generous Earned Income Tax Credit, universal health insurance, greater portability of pensions, and new ideas like wage-loss insurance would cushion the blow for workers who lose their jobs. All this should be uncontroversial. But, apparently, it is not.

Beyond that, the U.S. government must find ways to transform our inadequate social safety net into an effective social trampoline that bounces displaced workers back into productive employment—thereby helping the nation return to Lyndon Johnson's original Great Society concept: "a hand up, not a handout." According to the conventional wisdom, federal job training programs have a dismal track record. But in fact, their estimated rates of return have been quite respectable. The real problem is that, whether measured by the number of dollars spent or by the number of people served, we have never tried very hard. In evaluating these programs some years ago, LaLonde (1995, 149) concluded: "We got what we paid for. Public sector investments in training are exceedingly modest compared to [the problems they] are trying to address." And recent years have seen cutbacks. We simply must do better in the future.

Policy II: Preparing the Workforce of the Future

Ever since the late 1970s, the demand for labor appears to have been shifting away from high school graduates and dropouts and toward college graduates.[29] This shift, most economists believe, is the primary (though not the sole) reason for rising income inequality—dwarfing, for example, any effects of trade.[30] Economists have given this phenomenon an antiseptic name: skill-biased technical progress. It means that the labor market has turned ferociously against those with little education and low skills.

So far, America's response to this problem has not been to strengthen the social safety net, but to concentrate instead on keeping more young people in school longer (e.g., reducing high school dropouts and sending more kids to college) and improving the quality of schooling (e.g., via charter schools and No Child Left Behind). Success in these domains may have been modest, but it's not for lack of trying. Americans don't need to be reminded that education is important; the idea is etched into the public consciousness. Indeed, many people view education as the silver bullet. On hearing the question "How do we best prepare the American workforce of the future?," many Americans react reflexively with "Send more kids to college, and get more of them to study science and math."

Looking back over the past thirty years, that was probably excellent advice. But looking forward over the next thirty years, I suspect that more subtle educational advice will be needed. "Prepare our kids for the high-end personal service occupations that will not be offshored" is a more nuanced message than "keep them in school longer." But it may be more useful going forward. However, heeding that advice may require rethinking many aspects of our K–12 educational system in light of the new but critical distinction between personal and impersonal service jobs. As the First Industrial Revolution took hold, America radically transformed its educational system to meet the new demands of an industrial society. We may need to do something like that again.

In particular, I have argued that many impersonal service jobs will migrate offshore while personal service jobs will remain here. And it so happens that many well-paid jobs providing personal services—such as carpenters, electricians, and plumbers—do not require a college education. Others, like doctors, of course do. Overall, there is probably little or no correlation between the educational requirements of a job and its degree of offshorability.[31]

But before going even one sentence further, let me state categorically that I do *not* deny that raising the average educational attainment of the U.S. workforce is advisable ceteris paribus. On the contrary, to the extent that education raises productivity and that better-educated workers are more adaptable and/or more creative, educational investments should continue to pay off handsomely. In addition, inventiveness probably stands on a foundation of education—Bill Gates's famous decision to drop out of Harvard University notwithstanding. So it probably still makes sense to send more of America's youth to college. But over the next generation, what *kind* of education our young people receive may prove to be at least as important as *how much*. In that sense, a college degree may no longer be a panacea.

If this is so, what can we do about it? How can we prepare the workforce of the future for the brave new world of service offshoring—in which jobs in personal services grow relatively more abundant while jobs in impersonal services grow relatively more scarce? I am no educational expert, but let me offer a few ideas.

Starting in the elementary schools, we need to focus on developing our youngsters' imaginations, problem-solving skills, and people skills (including, importantly, group learning) as much as their "reading, writing, and 'rithmetic." Remember that grade you got on your kindergarten report card for "works and plays well with others"? It may become increasingly important as labor demand shifts toward personally delivered services. Such training probably needs to be continued and made more sophisticated in the secondary schools, where, for example, good communications skills—both written and verbal—need to be fostered. As one concrete example, it strikes me that the central thrust of No Child Left Behind is pushing American education in precisely the wrong direction. I am all for accountability. But the nation's school system will not build the creative, flexible, people-oriented workforce we will need in the future by force-feeding our kids rote preparation for standardized tests in the vain hope that they will perform as well as memory chips. They won't.

More vocational education is probably also in order. After all, nurses, carpenters, and plumbers are already scarce, and we will likely need relatively more of them in the future. Lately, I've been posing the following question to people:

"Twenty-five years from now, who do you think will earn more in America: the average computer programmer or the average carpenter?" You might be amazed that the overwhelming majority guess carpenter—which is also my guess. Much vocational training now takes place in community colleges; so they, too, will need to adapt their curricula to the job market of the future. For example, they may need to turn out fewer computer programmers and more computer repairers. (The Geek Squad probably has a great future!)

While it is probably still true that we should send more kids to college and get more of them to study science, math, and engineering, we also need to focus on training more college and graduate students for the high-end jobs that are unlikely to move offshore, and on developing a creative workforce that will keep America incubating and developing new processes, new products, and entirely new industries. Offshoring is, after all, mostly about following and copying. American must lead and innovate instead—just as we have done in the past. That remark leads me straight to the third, and final, basket.

Policy III: Climbing the Comparative Advantage Ladder

When I speak about offshoring, one straightforward but difficult question often comes up. "You claim that, in the future, we'll be importing many services that we now produce at home. But if imports grow rapidly, so must exports. What will America export?" It's a tough question. So perhaps I should opt for discretion over valor and simply hide behind a tautology: in the future, the United States will export the goods and services in which we have a comparative advantage! But let me venture just a bit beyond the realm of tautology.

For openers, I believe that service offshoring will exacerbate our already-large trade deficit, and that this imbalance will eventually drive down the value of the U.S. dollar. Trade theorists rarely mention *nominal* exchange rates, and open-economy macromodels typically assume that equilibrium *real* exchange rates do not change. I beg to differ. I believe that part of the United States' trade problem will be solved by a substantial real (and nominal) depreciation of the dollar, which will restore comparative advantage in places where we otherwise would lose it. The cost, of course, will be some diminution of the American standard of living.

Second, and related, service offshoring is a two-way street. The United States will not lose its comparative advantage in *all* the impersonal services that become increasingly tradable. I am thinking, for example, of the United States' strong competitive edge in finance, entertainment, and higher education. While none of them are impervious to foreign competition, Wall Street, Hollywood, and our great universities are not easily replicated abroad. And there are many other examples.

Third, it is crucial that the United States remain the incubator of new business ideas and the first mover when it comes to providing new goods and services. I like to use television sets as an example. The TV *manufacturing* industry really started here and at one point employed many workers. But as TV sets became "just a commodity," their production moved offshore to locations with much lower wages. And nowadays, the number of television sets manufactured in the United States is zero. A failure? No, a success. Like the cowboy hero, the leader innovates and moves on.

More important, we need to make sure that such success stories continue to proliferate—not because we prize the job destruction in the sunset industries that we lose, but because we value the job creation in the sunrise industries that we gain, even if those jobs won't stay here forever. Trying to name concrete examples of future industrial winners is a fool's errand, and I won't go there. Imagine yourself as Thomas Jefferson's chief economic adviser in 1802 (who should have been, but wasn't, Alexander Hamilton). You've just told the president that the share of Americans earning their living on farms will fall from 84 percent to 2 percent within 150–200 years—which would have been a remarkably prescient prediction. The great man looks worried, and asks: "And what will the other 82 percent do?" You couldn't have answered, but neither could anyone else.

While I'm not foolish enough to try to name the new industrial winners, we all know that many new goods and services will be invented and/or commercialized in the coming decades. As the world's leading nation, the United States must grab the first-mover advantage in a disproportionate share of these. And that, in turn, requires that we remain a hotbed of business creativity and innovation. To accomplish this, basic research, industrial R&D, creative and aggressive business management, an entrepreneurial culture, an active venture capital industry, and the like must all remain integral parts of the American success story. Thus, in short, a large part of the answer to the question "What will we export in the future?" is the new stuff.

An Offshoring Miscellany

Large-scale offshoring of impersonal service jobs from rich countries to poor countries will have numerous other implications, many of which we cannot even imagine now. But here are a few things that come to mind.

Slower Average Productivity Growth

If, in fact, the United States and other rich countries reallo-cate labor from manufacturing and impersonal service jobs, where there is rapid productivity improvement, to personal service jobs, where there is little or none, these nations' (weighted average) productivity growth rates will decline. Of course, the opposite reallocation will be going on in countries like India and China, boosting their productivity growth rates. This sectoral reallocation is a natural part of the international convergence process.[32]

The United States vs. Europe

The United States will probably cope with the necessary workplace and educational changes better than Europe, which has been talking much (but doing little) about fixing labor market "rigidities" for over a quarter century. Both history and logic suggest that markets, not governments, will play the lead role in effectuating the necessary shift of labor toward personally delivered services—and that markets will succeed. But the fluid, flexible American labor market will probably adapt better and faster than European labor markets will. On the other hand, the non-English-speaking countries of Europe will have less adapting to do because they will face less foreign competition in electroni-cally delivered services.[33]

China vs. India

Americans, and residents of other English-speaking coun-tries, probably need to start worrying less about competition from China, which is largely in manufactured goods, and more about competition from India, which is mainly in ser-vices. Speaking English is a notable source of comparative advantage that seems destined to grow in importance as impersonal services account for an increasing share of international trade. India has it. China does not—at least, not yet.[34]

Wage Inequality

Wage disparities between highly educated and poorly educated workers have grown alarmingly in the United States and in some other rich countries for decades. This phenomenon is largely blamed on skill-biased technical progress, which is widely expected to continue. But perhaps it will not. I have argued here that the rich-country jobs that are most vulnerable to offshoring, and thus will be under the greatest wage pressure in the future, are *not* mostly low-end jobs. They are jobs providing impersonal services, some of which now pay very high wages and some of which do not.

Need for New Data

Sadly, the national data systems of the United States and other industrial countries have not even fully adapted to the *First* Industrial Revolution yet. Governments all over the industrial world still devote vastly more resources to collecting agricultural data than the small size of that industry merits. So it can hardly be surprising that our data systems have failed to adapt to the Second Industrial Revolution— the shift to services. Throughout the world, there is far less information on the service sector (which is the majority everywhere) than on manufacturing (which is the minority). The Third Industrial Revolution demands not only that we keep better statistical tabs on services, but that we start collecting systematic data on which service jobs are deliverable electronically over long distances and which are not. Needless to say, no one is doing this now. It will be hard even to assess the size and nature of the offshoring problem, much less to do anything constructive about it, in the absence of such data.

Job Satisfaction

I close my potpourri on an optimistic note, with a highly conjectural possible side effect of the coming shift from manufacturing and impersonal services to personal services. Human beings are social animals who enjoy human contact. For many decades, it looked as if modern economic life was destined to reduce the volume of human contact in the workplace—separating people and isolating them. (Remember Charlie Chaplin in *Modern Times*?) In future decades, that trend may reverse in the rich countries, as personal services come to predominate more, possibly leading to less alienation and greater average job satisfaction.

A Recapitulation

Let me conclude by summarizing the basic argument as crisply as I can, leaving out all the details and nuances:

• Thanks to electronic communications and globalization, the future is likely to see much more offshoring of *impersonal services*, that is, services that can be delivered electronically from afar with little or no degradation of quality.

• Thanks to the emergence of China, the former Soviet bloc, and especially India, there will be a lot more workers available to do these jobs. This new expansion of international trade will raise world welfare, and we should not try to stop it with protectionism.

• Service offshoring may eventually amount to a Third Industrial Revolution, and industrial revolutions have a way of transforming societies. For openers, rich countries will need to shift sizable portions of their workforces out of impersonal services and manufacturing and into personal services—and to train their workforces accordingly.

• That said, the "threat" from offshoring should not be exaggerated. Just as the First Industrial Revolution did not banish agriculture from the rich countries, and the Second Industrial Revolution has not banished manufacturing, the Third Industrial Revolution will not drive all impersonal services offshore. Nor will it lead to mass unemployment. But the necessary adjustments will be large, multifaceted, and complex. In a word, it's likely to be a big deal.

• The societies of the rich countries seem to be completely unprepared for the coming industrial transformation. Our national data systems, our trade policies, our educational systems, our social welfare programs, our politics, and much else must adapt to the fundamental movement from impersonal to personal service jobs. None of this is happening now.

When I talk to my fellow economists about offshoring, I often feel a bit like Paul Revere sounding the alarm to awaken his slumbering neighbors—except that many of my intellectual neighbors do not appreciate being rousted out of bed. And this time it's not the British who are coming, but the Indians. And they are coming neither by land nor by sea, but electronically. And, by the way, we certainly *don't* want to fight them off. (So please stay right here; don't rush off to Lexington or Concord.)

In particular, we Americans should not blame the Indians for the large adjustment problems that we will have to confront in the coming decades. They are doing exactly what they should be doing—developing their own country by exploiting their comparative advantage and, in the process, making the world as a whole immensely better off. We should shake their hands and wish them well—which is not exactly how the Minutemen greeted the Redcoats.

Notes

This paper was presented at the Alvin Hansen Symposium at Harvard University, May 2, 2007. I would like to thank, without implicating, Gene Grossman, Helmut Wagner, and an anonymous reviewer for helpful comments on an earlier draft, Lael Brainard and Alan Krueger for valuable references, and Princeton's Center for Economic Policy Studies for financial support. I am also grateful for many useful comments from colleagues on several earlier papers on this subject.

1. There is no issue over whether or not offshoring is a positive development for the world as a whole. We all agree that it is.

2. Or so we think. In January 2008, the National Public Radio show *Marketplace* carried a story about remote monitoring of patients in intensive care units! Since lawn care requires the gardener's physical presence, it appears to be a quintessentially personal service. But a Chinese-American businessman told me about a company that is developing technology to operate a lawn mower electronically from China. The beat goes on.

3. Levy and Yu (2006) show that offshoring of radiological services is severely restricted by regulation. So large-scale offshoring in this domain would require regulatory changes. Technology is not the limiting factor.

4. According to the BLS's payroll survey, 83.4 percent of U.S. jobs in 2006 were producing services—if we count all government jobs as service jobs.

5. Bhagwati, Panagariya, and Srinivasan entitled their 2004 paper "The Muddles over Outsourcing." (They meant offshoring.)

6. In fact, ever since my stint in government in the 1990s, many people have heard me say that my personal views on trade policy are somewhat to the right of Jagdish Bhagwati! Maybe that's not true any more.

7. See Bhagwati 1968, Gomory and Baumol 2000, and Samuelson 2004.

8. This is a *prospective* possibility. It recent years, the U.S. terms of trade have improved, not deteriorated.

9. See, for example, Davidson and Matusz (2000), who criticize standard trade theory for this reason.

10. Hypermetromia is the opposite of myopia.

11. See, for example, the summary of estimates in the National Academy of Public Administration 2006 (chapter 4). Job losses in manufacturing, which started years earlier, have been much larger.

12. Among many references that could be cited, see Baumol 1967.

13. Nordhaus (2006) offers extensive empirical support for these and other predictions of Baumol's disease.

14. Robert Z. Lawrence (this volume, chapter 3) suggests that many of the most important personal services, such as health care and education, do in fact have high income elasticities. More on this later.

15. This point is emphasized by Grossman and Rossi-Hansberg (2006).

16. One economist to whom I posed this question suggested that, by then, the students "in the seats" might also be holograms! Of course, the United States might also "onshore" some college teaching services if foreign students tune in to our lectures.

17. Several other authors have attempted to do this, too, using different methodologies. See, among others, Bardhan and Kroll (2003) and Kletzer (2006).

18. For an explanation of how I tried to do this, and why it failed, see Blinder 2008 (section 5).

19. The pronounced spike in the 66–70 range reflects my arbitrary decision to place most manufacturing jobs there. It is of no importance because all candidate dividing lines fall to the left of it. (Thus manufacturing jobs are considered potentially offshorable.) Similarly, the huge pileup in the 1–25 range reflects my decision not to bother ranking jobs that are clearly not offshorable. Thus, for example, I made no effort to decide which of these jobs was a "1" and which was a "24" because the dividing line would never be drawn that low.

20. Davidson and Matusz (2006) chide trade theorists for ignoring this obvious fact. They suggest that omitting job churn leads to highly misleading conclusions in trade models.

21. Offshoring is, of course, not the only reason, nor even the main reason, for any of these three types of unemployment.

22. Of course, other phenomena—like invention and innovation—will produce more job creation than destruction.

23. See Blinder 2008 for why $n = 291$ in this regression. I have no measure of average years of experience by occupation. The R^2 of the regression is 0.61 and the RMSE is 0.26.

24. In case you are thinking otherwise, *ED* and the offshoring dummies are nearly orthogonal.

25. The Hansen debate took place in May 2007, when the U.S. unemployment rate was 4.5 percent. At this revision (January 2009), the unemployment rate is up to 7.2 percent and rising.

26. Chinese-speaking Singapore and Taiwan may have even bigger adjustments to make. But they are small countries.

27. As I noted earlier, this is not really a theorem. There are cases where the losses exceed the gains.

28. As an example of the latter, the Trade Adjustment Assistance and Reform Act of 2002 created a small wage-loss insurance program for workers above a certain age who lose their jobs to import competition or offshoring. But so far, it has been taken up by fewer than seven thousand workers.

29. This section borrows heavily from Blinder 2006b.

30. See, for example, Burtless 1995.

31. For empirical evidence supporting this point, see Blinder 2008.

32. See, for example, Baumol, Batey Blackman, and Wolff 1989.

33. Less, but not zero. In many occupations, cheaper labor in Eastern Europe can provide electronic services to businesses in Western Europe. There are Polish plumbers, but there are also Polish computer programmers.

34. It is a good bet that the English-language skills of the Chinese workforce will improve over the coming decades. In addition, deficiencies in English may not be terribly important in some technical jobs (e.g., computer programming).

References

Atkinson, Robert D. 2006. "Apocalypse Soon? Why Alan Blinder Gets It Wrong on Offshoring." Washington, DC: The Information Technology and Innovation Foundation.

Bardhan, Ashok Deo, and Cynthia Kroll. 2003. "The New Wave of Outsourcing." Fisher Center Research Report #1103. November.

Baumol, William J. 1967. "Macroeconomics of Unbalanced Growth: The Anatomy of Urban Crisis." *American Economic Review* 57, no. 3 (June): 415–426.

Baumol, William J., Sue Anne Batey Blackman, and Edward N. Wolff. 1989. *Productivity and American Leadership: The Long View.* Cambridge, MA: MIT Press.

Bhagwati, Jagdish N. 1968. "Distortions and Immiserizing Growth: A Generalization." *Review of Economic Studies* 35, no. 4: 481–485.

Bhagwati, Jagdish N. 1997. "A New Epoch?" *The New Republic* (May 19, 1997): 36–41. Reprinted in his *A Stream of Windows: Unsettling Reflections on Trade, Immigration, and Democracy,* 3–28. Cambridge, MA: The MIT Press, 1998.

Bhagwati, Jagdish, Arvind Panagariya, and T. N. Srinivasan. 2004. "The Muddles over Outsourcing." *Journal of Economic Perspectives* 18, no. 4 (Fall): 93–114.

Blinder, Alan S. 2006a. "Offshoring: The Next Industrial Revolution?" *Foreign Affairs* 85, no. 2 (March–April): 113–128.

Blinder, Alan S. 2006b. "Outsourcing: Bigger Than You Thought." *The American Prospect* 17, no. 11 (November): 44–46.

Blinder, Alan S. 2008. "How Many U.S. Jobs Might Be Offshorable?" Princeton University working paper.

Burtless, Gary. 1995. "International Trade and the Rise in Earnings Inequality." *Journal of Economic Literature* 23 (June): 800–816.

Davidson, Carl, and Steven J. Matusz. 2000. "Globalisation and Labour-Market Adjustment: How Fast and at What Cost?" *Oxford Review of Economic Policy* 16, no. 3 (Autumn): 42–56.

Davidson, Carl, and Steven J. Matusz. 2006. "Trade Liberalization and Compensation." *International Economic Review* 47, no. 3 (August): 723–747.

Freeman, Richard. 2005. "What Really Ails Europe (and America): The Doubling of the Global Workforce." *The Globalist*, June 3. www.theglobalist.com. Washington, DC.

Gomory, Ralph E., and William J. Baumol. 2000. *Global Trade and Conflicting National Interests*. Cambridge, MA: MIT Press.

Grossman, Gene M., and Esteban Rossi-Hansberg. August 2006. "Trading Tasks: A Simple Theory of Offshoring." Princeton University working paper.

Hymans, Saul, and Frank Stafford. 1995. "Divergence, Convergence, and the Gains from Trade." *Review of International Economics* 3, no. 1: 118–123.

Kletzer, Lori G. 2006. "The Scope of Tradable Services and the Task Content of Offshorable Services Jobs." University of California, Santa Cruz. April.

LaLonde, Robert J. 1995. "The Promise of Public Sector-Sponsored Training Programs." *Journal of Economic Perspectives* 9, no. 2 (Spring): 149–168.

Levy, Frank, and Kyoung-Hee Yu. March 2006. "Offshoring of Professional Services: Radiology Services from India." MIT working paper. March.

Mankiw, N. Gregory, and Phillip Swagel. 2006. "The Politics and Economics of Offshore Outsourcing." NBER working paper no. 12398. July.

National Academy of Public Administration. 2006. *Off-Shoring: An Elusive Phenomenon*. Academy Project no. 2051-000. Washington, DC. January.

Nordhaus, William D. 2006. "Baumol's Diseases: A Macroeconomic Perspective." NBER working paper no. 12218. May.

Samuelson, Paul A. 2004. "Where Ricardo and Mill Rebut and Confirm Arguments of Mainstream Economists Supporting Globalization." *Journal of Economic Perspectives* 18, no. 3 (Summer): 135–146.

3 Comments

RICHARD B. FREEMAN

During the early 1990s debate over trade and the North American Free Trade Agreement (NAFTA), many economists assured Americans that we had lots to gain and little to lose. Globalization would bring high-wage skilled jobs to the United States and send low-wage unskilled jobs to Mexico and other low-income trading partners. Opponents of NAFTA worried that U.S. firms would move manufacturing facilities overseas and that increased trade would drive down the wages of less-educated Americans. Few on either side of the debate believed that U.S. firms would offshore "good" jobs to Mexico or other low-wage countries. After all, the workforces in those countries were less educated than ours.

What a difference a decade makes! Arguments about the benefits/costs of globalization no longer focus on low skill manufacturing jobs but on the offshoring of traditional non-tradable service-sector work (http:/en.wikipedia.org/wiki/Offshoring). Offshoring surfaced briefly during the 2004 election campaign when Democratic Party candidate John Kerry denounced "Benedict Arnold CEOs" for moving facilities overseas (VandeHei 2004), but Kerry never followed up this statement, seemingly silenced by his financial backers and economic advisors. During the campaign many in the business community denied that offshoring was significant. Some analysts cited BLS data on the causes of job loss that the agency had never designed to estimate jobs moved overseas as showing that offshoring was negligible.

Today, firms do not deny reality. U.S.-based multinationals proudly declare that they are global firms ready and eager to move work to wherever they can hire cheap labor. Check the Offshoring Institute on the Internet (https://www.offshoring_institute.org/) or the McKinsey Global Institute (http://www.mckinsey.com/mgi/rp/offshoring/). If you can raise profits by sending or threatening to send jobs overseas, you better do so or else you may face a takeover bid by someone who will increase profits through the offshoring card.

The U.K. Institute of Directors has the clearest statement of the reality of offshoring, albeit referring to the United Kingdom rather than the United States:

The availability of high-speed, low-cost communications, coupled with the rise in high-level skills in developing countries meant offshoring has become an attractive option outside the manufacturing industry. Britain has seen call centres and IT support move away from Britain, but now creative services such as design and advertising work are being outsourced. There is more to come. In theory, anything that does not demand physical contact with a customer can be outsourced to anywhere on the globe. For many UK businesses this presents new opportunities, for others it represents a serious threat. But welcome it or fear it, it is happening anyway, and we had better get used to it. (Institute of Directors, reported in www.politics.co.uk, 2006)

Getting used to it, American workers express great concerns about offshoring. In 2004 an Employment Law Alliance survey found that 6 percent of workers claimed to have lost a job because their work was sent overseas; 10 percent said that they feared losing their job due to it being sent to an overseas subcontractor; and 30 percent reported that someone they knew had lost a job due to offshoring. An Associated Press-IPSOS survey in the same year reported that 20 percent of Americans said that they, a family member, or someone they knew personally lost a job due to offshoring (www.danieldrezner.com/archives/001355.html).

Why Offshoring Now?

Three forces have made offshoring a reality in globalization.

First is the advent of China, India, and the ex–Soviet bloc countries to the global capitalist system. When these countries joined the global economy in the 1990s, they added 1.3 billion or so workers to the global workforce, effectively doubling the number of workers in the world economy. At the same time, these countries added little to the world's stock of useful capital. The big influx of labor and modest influx of capital reduced the global capital labor ratio and shifted the balance of power in the labor market toward firms (Freeman 2005a, b; 2007). With a new huge supply of low-wage labor, American multinationals and those of other countries had a powerful tool with which to beat down pressures for rising wages.

The second factor is the massive growth of higher education in developing countries—particularly, China and India. From the 1990s through the mid-2000s, enrollments in higher education increased rapidly in low-wage countries—particularly China (Freeman 2008). By the mid-2000s, China was graduating four million plus bachelor's degree graduates annually while India graduated over one million. This greatly expanded the supply of low-wage workers with sufficient education for working in "call centres and IT support . . . creative services such as design and advertising . . . anything that does not demand physical contact with a customer."

The third factor contributing to offshoring is technological: the digitalization of white-collar work and transfer of computer and Internet technology to developing countries. Digitalization means that many office-type jobs can be done at any locale connected to the global information technology communications network. The transfer of technology to developing countries means that workers in those countries can compete in more work activities with workers in advanced countries.

The doubling of the global labor force, investment in education in low-wage countries, and digitalization of work seemingly makes offshoring inevitable, although no one foresaw this during the early 1990s globalization debates. So much for the prescience of economists and policy analysts about the economics of globalization.

How Many Jobs Are Offshorable?

How many jobs involve "anything that does not demand physical contact with a customer"? Will your job be offshored to a low-wage worker in the near future? Blinder estimates that on the order of 30–40 percent of U.S. jobs are potentially offshorable—leading him to call this a "new industrial revolution" (Blinder 2006). Some may view this assessment as alarmist, but it more likely understates than overstates the number of potentially moveable jobs. He argues that while "impersonal service jobs will leave, personal service jobs will remain," whereas technology permits both sorts of jobs to shift to lower-cost workers and locales.

Consider, for instance, medical services that require face-to-face diagnosis and care—a high-level personal service. Doctors in low-wage countries cannot send hospital services or conduct surgery over the Internet, but they can deliver those services to patients via "health tourism" (http://www.india4health.com). In 2006 the Steelworkers Union objected to having its members travel to India for hospital operations despite the high quality and low cost (Rai 2006).

Blinder's estimate of the number of jobs that are potentially offshorable is judgmental. Brad Jensen and Lori Kletzer (2006) use the geographic distribution of employment in the United States to obtain an objective measure of the potential movability of U.S. jobs. They argue that service-sector jobs that are geographically concentrated in the United States could just as easily be concentrated outside the country. On the basis of the uneven distribution of service jobs in the United States, they estimate that about 30 percent of U.S. employment is vulnerable to offshoring—which is of the same order of magnitude as Blinder's assessment.

But Isn't All for the Best in the Best of All Possible Worlds?

Is the offshoring of good white-collar jobs good or bad for the United States and American labor?

Some economists see offshoring as part of trade, whose positive impacts on the economy override any negative impacts on particular groups (Mankiw and Swagel 2005; Mann 2006; Farrell 2006). Viewing offshoring as akin to a productivity advance, Grossman and Rossi-Hansber (2006) argue that the benefits accrue disproportionately to workers in offshorable activities (by raising their productivity) and that offshoring benefits native workers more than would a comparable flow of immigrants. Others (Gomory and Baumol 2000; Samuelson 2004) note that the transfer of technology from advanced countries to lower-income countries can harm the economy of the advanced country (through loss of its monopoly on the advanced technology and reduced price of the output). Markusen (2005) has developed models that allow for both gains and losses from offshoring. Labor specialists estimate that workers typically suffer a 20 percent loss of earnings when they are laid off, for reasons of trade, offshoring, or anything else, so that an assessment of welfare cannot dismiss adjustment costs as trivial.

Overall, the general presumption is that offshoring (like globalization in general) raises national and world output but harms some workers. Thus, the key questions for assessing offshoring are empirical: who does it benefit by how much, who does it harm by how much, and the extent to which the social safety net limits the cost to those who suffer harm.

Given the unexpected rise of offshoring and public concern over what it may do to worker well-being, it is important to understand the conditions under which we should welcome or fear it, and the policies that will best protect U.S. workers from this seeming threat to their well-being. For all their charm, the sound-bite quips, insider jokes, and references to diverse celebrities, economists, and journalists (three Pauls [McCartney, Samuelson, Krugman], Hillary Clinton, William Greider, Charlie Rose, Paul Craig Roberts, as well as diverse others) in Bhagwati's chapter do little to illuminate the issues or respond to criticisms of the current form of globalization.

What does Bhagwati think about the issues that arouse concern: the unexpected rise in inequality in developing countries; the slowdown in world economic growth during this era of rapid globalization; the rising proportion of workers in informal sector employment—the realities that have led the World Bank and the International Monetary Fund (IMF) to back off from their expansive claims for Washington Consensus globalization policies? What sort of evidence, if any, should convince us to accept or reject the view that the current form of globalization has "gone too far"? Are 30 percent of jobs offshorable worthy of attention? If not 30 percent, how about 60 percent? Is potential loss of U.S. comparative advantage in high-tech industries worth worrying about or not? If 20 percent of the drop in the real earnings of U.S. workers or of the rise of inequality is due to globalization, should we reassess economic policies? How about if 80 percent is attributable to globalization?

Bhagwati appears to attribute growing skepticism toward globalization largely to a media frenzy stoked by journalists who exaggerate the disagreements of economists over the benefits and costs of trade. I disagree with this interpretation. Most Americans judge economic reality from what they observe in their lives, not from debates among economists or what journalists write. The reality includes job losses and threats of job losses due to offshoring and trade, three decades of stagnant real wages for most workers despite rapid productivity growth, and greater inequality, to which globalization contributed. The reality is that the world has begun a huge transition toward a global labor market that will greatly benefit the vast majority of persons but that will create problems for many workers in high-wage countries (Freeman 2007). The debate over offshoring and globalization needs the kind of respectful discussion of this transition that Blinder has assayed.

What Might We Do If We Worry?

Given Blinder's claim that offshoring will have a sizable impact on the U.S. job market, I expected that he would roll out a radical set of policy recommendations. Tax the rich more, as Warren Buffett has suggested. Invest massively in infrastructure. Use the tax system to direct corporate investments to the United States. Support nanotechnology or whatever we think may underlie the industries of the future (though call it something other than industrial policy). Blinder's policy suggestions are surprisingly modest. Yes, the United States could improve its safety net for workers who lose jobs, but the Trade Adjustment Assistance (TAA) program has never been effective, and I doubt that a wage insurance scheme will do all that much either. I am dubious that more spending on education, vocation training, and the like will do much to reduce the country's high levels of inequality. I favor increased investment in science and engineering but doubt that this will spill over much to help those in the middle or bottom of the income distribution as long as multinationals send production overseas.

Given that globalization has weakened the bargaining position of workers, I believe that the country needs an aggressive set of policies to (1) strengthen the institutions that represent normal workers in their dealings with management—trade unions and other worker organizations; (2) increase the basket of nonmarket goods and services and guaranteed level of income for all citizens regardless of how they fare in the labor market, such as an increased Earned Income Tax Credit, national health insurance, pension reforms, and increased spending on infrastructure and the environment; (3) raise the share of capital income that accrues to ordinary citizens through greater profit sharing, employee stock ownership, pension fund ownership of firms; (4) reform corporate governance so that workers and shareholders have greater say; (5) increase research and development spending in areas likely to gain comparative advantage in the next several decades.

Between 1990 and 2006, GDP per capita grew by 1.9 percent per year in the United States. This raised income per head by $11,300 over the period. Given the greater initial level of GDP per capita in the United States than in China (measured with purchasing power parity price indices), income per head rose by nearly twice as much in absolute terms in the United States than in China, despite China's 8.9 percent growth rate of GDP per capita. If globalization and offshoring harmed economic growth in the United States, this does not show up in these statistics. Had the increased GDP per capita gone proportionately to every person—preserving the distribution of income that existed in 1990—every family of four would have gained about $45,000 more in family income. With such a distribution of the benefits of economic growth, I would expect that most American workers would be on the bandwagon of globalization. To paraphrase Shakespeare's Cassius (*Julius Caesar*, act 1, scene 2):

The fault, dear Brutus, is not in offshoring or globalization,
But in ourselves, that we are underlings
Unwilling to lean against the market winds
When they favor powerful moneyed kings.

References

Blinder, Alan S. 2006. "Offshoring: The Next Industrial Revolution?" *Foreign Affairs* 85, no. 2 (March–April): 113–128.

Farrell, Diana. 2006. "Don't Be Afraid of Offshoring." *Business Week Online.* March 22. http://www.businessweek.com/globalbiz/content/mar2006/gb20060322_649013.htm.

Freeman, Richard. 2005a. "The Great Doubling: America in the New Global Economy." Usery Lecture, Georgia State University, April 8.

Freeman, Richard. 2005b. "What Really Ails Europe (and America): The Doubling of the Global Workforce." *The Globalist,* June 3. http://www.theglobalist.com/StoryId.aspx?StoryId=4542.

Freeman, Richard B. 2007. "The Challenge of the Growing Globalization of Labor Markets to Economic and Social Policy." Chapter 2 in Eva Pau, ed., *Global Capitalism Unbound.* London: Palgrave MacMillan.

Freeman, Richard B. 2008. "What Does the Growth of Higher Education Overseas Mean for the U.S." Paper presented at the NBER Conference on American Universities in a Global Market, October 2–4. Forthcoming in *American Universities in a Global Market,* ed. Charles T. Clotfelter (Chicago: University of Chicago Press).

Gomory, Ralph, and William Baumol. 2000. *Global Trade and Conflicting National Interest.* Cambridge, MA: MIT Press.

Grossman, Gene M., and Esteban Rossi-Hansberg. 2006. "Trading Tasks: A Simple Theory of Offshoring." NBER working paper no. 12721. December.

Jensen, J. Bradford, and Lori G. Kletzer. 2006. "Tradable Services: Understanding the Scope and Impact of Services Offshoring." In Susan Collins and Lael Brainard, eds., *Brookings Trade Forum 2005: Offshoring White-Collar Work,* 75–134. Washington, DC: Brookings Institution.

Mankiw, N. Gregory, and Philip Swagel. 2005. "The Politics and Economics of Offshore Outsourcing." November 9. http://www.ssc.wisc.edu/~mchinn/outsourcing_MankiwSwagel.pdf.

Mann, Catherine. 2006. *Accelerating the Globalization of America: The Role for Information Technology.* Washington, DC: Institute for International Economics. June.

Markusen, James. 2005. "Modeling the Offshoring of White-Collar Services: From Comparative Advantage to the New Theories of Trade and FDI," in Susan Collins and Lael Brainard, eds., *Brookings Trade Forum 2005, Offshoring White-Collar Work: The Issues and Implications.* Washington, DC: Brookings Institution.

Rai, Saritha. 2006. Union Disrupts Plan to Send Ailing Workers to India for Cheaper Medical Care. *New York Times,* October 11. http://

www.nytimes.com/2006/10/11/business/worldbusiness/11health .html?_r=1&ref=health&oref=slogin.

Samuelson, Paul A. 2004. "Where Ricardo and Mill Rebut and Confirm Arguments of Mainstream Economists Supporting Globalization." *Journal of Economic Perspectives* 18, no 3 (Summer 2004): 135–146.

VandeHei, Jim. 2004. "Kerry Donors Include 'Benedict Arnolds': Candidate Decries Tax-Haven Firms While Accepting Executives' Aid. *Washington Post*, February 26, A01. http://www.washingtonpost.com/wp_dyn/articles/ A6884_2004Feb25.html.

DOUGLAS A. IRWIN

The two chapters presented at this debate are quite different. Alan S. Blinder suggests that offshoring of white-collar jobs will create major problems for the U.S. economy in coming years, whereas Jagdish Bhagwati provides a sketch of recent trade "problems" that have captured the media's attention but have lacked much substance.

Bhagwati notes that economists can spark a media frenzy—to the extent that our profession is capable of generating such a thing—by making controversial arguments that seem to have some negative implications for "free-trade" policies, either theoretically conceived or actually practiced. Any economist suggesting that Japan posed a menace to high-technology industries in the United States in the 1980s, or that China's rise threatens our standards of living today, or that India and the Internet are poised to erase our high-paying white-collar jobs tomorrow, are bound to attract attention. Bhagwati observes that these episodes come and go, comparing them to balloons that eventually lose their helium, but not before they generate stories in the press about "new doubts about free trade." In the end, the concerns eventually pass from the scene while leaving the credibility of free trade among economists largely intact.

I am quite sympathetic to Bhagwati's view on this. In my book *Against the Tide: An Intellectual History of Free Trade* (1996), I chronicle the numerous theoretical attacks made against free trade since the time of Adam Smith. Some of the attacks have qualified the case for free trade, but they never really undermined it. In a similar way, contemporary fears about trade raised by non-economists also tend to fade away with time. During the NAFTA debate in the early 1990s, Ross Perot raised the specter of a "giant sucking sound" of American jobs leaving for Mexico. One hears as much about this problem these days as one hears about the threat that Japan poses for the future livelihood of our children.

But Alan S. Blinder, a distinguished and sensible economist, has resurrected Perot-esque fear about offshoring and India. He would probably deny this charge. In his *Foreign Affairs* article, Blinder (2006) wrote: "We should not view the coming wave of offshoring as an impending catastrophe." In his remarks at this conference, he reiterated that his was not "a forecast of impending doom."

Yet in his chapter for this debate, Blinder comes pretty close to implying that offshoring will be an impending catastrophe. Just read his description of the effects of offshoring: "Adjustment to offshoring will be of major magnitude, will last a long time, and will create millions of losers" . . . The transition will be "massive and disruptive" and "nasty". . . . "historically unprecedented" . . . "large and potentially disruptive force for the United States" leading to a "massive, lengthy, and painful transition as millions of workers are rudely reallocated by the unforgiving market."

These are pretty dire predictions. Perhaps he is just trying to get our attention. As John Maynard Keynes opined, "Words ought to be a little wild for they are the assaults of thought on the unthinking." If so, he has succeeded.

Blinder's chapter is an admirably clear discussion of the threat of outsourcing. He sweeps away many of the things that are sometimes brought up in the context of the offshoring debate: he does not question whether comparative advantage is obsolete, or whether we need a new paradigm in trade theory, or whether the U.S. terms of trade might deteriorate as China develops, or whether the United States might lose important and strategic industries. We could talk about each of these points, but they muddy the water and distract from Blinder's key concern.

His key concern is that thirty to forty million American jobs are potentially offshorable, and the gross job losses "will be huge, leading to a great deal of churning, much displacement (and reemployment) of labor, and many difficult adjustments."

He makes all the standard qualifications that economists usually make, agreeing that trade is a two-way street, arguing that free trade remains the best policy, stressing that the issue is not about the overall number of jobs (net employment). Even so, he is pretty pessimistic: even if the economy remains at full employment, the labor market churn will increase and "offshoring per se will lead to far more job destruction than job creation in the United States." In addition, it will create a "new class of trade victims"—namely white-collar professionals.

Let it not go unremarked that the one thing that is missing from this entire scenario is *evidence*. The United States is a large *net exporter* of services and many business services have been outsourced to it—even from places like India. The

United States has a strong comparative advantage in many of these service sectors, and technological changes create many opportunities for U.S. service firms in foreign markets. So do we really know that offshoring will create more destruction than creation? No. As he honestly and repeatedly admits, we are speculating about the future, and we don't know how things are going to turn out. Could he be right? Sure! Could he be wrong? Yes, I think that he would admit to that possibility, and if he won't then I'll admit it for him.

But the answer is a little bit better than "we don't know." Blinder does not cite the work of Mary Amiti and Shang-Jin Wei (2005), Jacob Kirkegaard (2007), and others who have crunched some numbers and conclude that the disruption may not be as great as he anticipates. If they are wrong in their analysis, it would be interesting to hear Blinder's critique.

But rather than engage in a debate about the numbers, all of which are fairly speculative, I wish to make a few general points. As I read Blinder's bleak prognosis, I thought back to two phrases that we associate with Alfred Marshall.

The first is the *"natura non facit saltum,"* or "nature makes no leap," which is the epigraph of Marshall's great *Principles of Economics* in 1890. It could be the case that offshoring proves to be as large a phenomenon as Blinder anticipates. But whether it is *disruptive* as he expects depends entirely on the time scale over which it occurs. Blinder implies that it is all very imminent and will take place on a large scale very soon. (Although the opportunity is there and the technology exists for offshoring, we haven't seen it yet—but just you wait!) No doubt, if there is a sudden surge of offshoring of the magnitude he anticipates, it will be very disruptive.

But I think it is more likely that offshoring will play out over several decades, implying no immediate disruption but a slower longer-term adjustment. And the longer the off-shoring phenomenon plays out, the easier it will be for U.S. labor markets to absorb its impact. So it is possible to have large numbers of American jobs offshored in the end and yet for the process be a relatively smooth one. As he points out, four million American workers gain or lose a job each month. So in one month, U.S. labor markets churn 10 percent of his gross figure. If we spread his gross figure out over three or four decades, the magnitude of the problem dwindles significantly.

The implicit vision that Blinder creates is big-time downsizing, all at once. But there are many ways in which labor markets adjust. Think back to how the U.S. manufacturing sector adjusted to foreign competition in the 1970s and 1980s. Only part of the adjustment was through abrupt, massive layoffs, and then mainly due to the severe recession in 1981–1982. A good deal of the employment adjustment was through attrition and labor turnover—simply not hiring new workers when existing workers retired or left for another job. It was the new entrants to the labor market who did some of the adjusting by simply finding that there were no jobs available in old sectors (they simply were not hiring), and instead one had to move to another sector of the economy.

Another form of adjustment was the repositioning of firms in product markets, moving toward higher-quality, higher-value-added, niche markets. The spread of manufacturing around the world has led to massive two-way trade in manufactured goods across countries. As capabilities in services spread around the world, there will probably be a much more refined division of labor in that sector accompanied by large-scale two-way trade in services. That does not automatically imply mass layoffs, but rather workers doing different things within the service sector. The process in manufacturing was not abrupt, but has taken many years to work out and indeed is continual—and ongoing.

The other Alfred Marshall phrase that came to mind is the analogy that, just as both blades of a pair of scissors are responsible for cutting a sheet of paper, both the supply and the demand curve are responsible for the determination of price. Blinder is careful to say that thirty to forty million is the number of jobs that are *potentially* offshorable, not an estimate of the number that actually will be offshored. The number that *will* be offshored depends also upon the number of people in foreign countries—India, in particular—who are capable of supplying the work right now that is potentially offshorable from the United States. In the popular imagination, the foreign supply curve is perfectly elastic at prevailing wages.

And yet there is clear evidence that the foreign supply curve is upward sloping. The evidence is the double-digit annual increase in wages in India and elsewhere for skilled workers who do the outsourced work. As these wages rise, the potential gains from outsourcing are narrowed. Blinder says very little about the binding supply constraints abroad. The number of Indian and Chinese workers is enormous, but the real number of those ready to provide services at world-class standards is much smaller. Of course, the long-run supply is much more elastic from these countries, but that is precisely my point—it will take a great deal of time to work out the problems in India's educational system to bring into play larger numbers of potential workers, diminishing offshoring as an imminent threat.

Indeed, an article in the *New York Times* on May 24, 2007, points to two factors that will mitigate the gains from offshoring to India: the appreciation of the rupee against the dollar, and the double-digit rise in wage rates in India.[1] Both limit the benefits of one-sided outsourcing to India. Another article in the *New York Times* on September 25, 2007, entitled "Outsourcing Works So Well, India Is Sending Jobs Abroad," talks about the consequences: Wipro and other Indian firms are outsourcing some work to "underdeveloped" parts of the United States, such as Idaho and Georgia, because it is cheaper to do it there.

Therefore, a plausible case can be made that nature makes no leap and the adjustment will be steady and unrelenting, but drawn out and manageable.

As a huge fan of Blinder's splendid book *Hard Heads, Soft Hearts*, I regret that, in raising the specter of massive outsourcing, he now misses what I regard as a "teachable moment." When Perot claimed that NAFTA would generate a "giant sucking sound" of American jobs going to Mexico, that was a teachable moment for economists—an opportunity to join the debate and temper the exaggerated fears.

There is already a great deal of concern out there about India and China and a lot of hype about offshoring. This is a teachable moment for economists. To me, the most important sentence in Blinder's provocative chapter is this: "Open, flexible labor markets do a remarkably good job of handling large-scale reallocations." That is an important message that is buried in this chapter (see also Brown, Haltiwanger, and Lane 2006, and Baumol 2002).

Let me turn briefly to policy remedies.

Blinder talks about three policy responses—building a better safety net, preparing the workforce for the future, and climbing the ladder of comparative advantage. So essentially this comes down to—more and better compensation for displaced workers, strengthening the education system, and encouraging new business growth and the creation of higher- skilled jobs.

My reaction is this: after getting us all excited about offshoring, he offers us plain-vanilla remedies. This triad of better compensation, more education, and improved upgrading is something of a mantra among economists, something that economists of all stripes can support and have been preaching for decades. These are the standard arguments that economists resort to after identifying the trade problem du jour, whether it was the rise of multinationals in the 1970s, trade with Japan in the 1980s, the response to NAFTA in the 1990s, and so forth. There is nothing new here, and I think the reason is that there is an inescapable reality here: there are no easy policies to recommend.

Consider trade adjustment assistance. The budgetary costs of TAA are trivial in comparison with the gains from trade. I suspect that most economists consider TAA to be grossly underfunded and would be happy to see it expanded by a factor of five or ten. But the problem is as much how to design TAA and other compensation programs as it is to expand the size of them. A problem with the current system is that the payment is tied to the length of the unemployment spell, thereby encouraging the recipient to remain unemployed. Suppose TAA is paid out (say, $50,000) as one lump sum upon displacement: would that really allay people's concerns about globalization risk? The labor movement has been skeptical of TAA for some time, ever since the early 1970s when AFL-CIO president George Meany dismissed it as "burial insurance." Another recent proposal to improve TAA is to provide wage insurance, wherein compensation is tied to a portion of the pre-layoff wage. But if Blinder is correct and it is high-wage white-collar professionals who are most at risk from offshoring, then wage insurance will not be of much help—it is doubtful that there will be much political support for a highly regressive transfer policy to compensate someone (radiologists earning $500,000?) for their temporary displacement.

As for education, that is a huge topic unto itself. Blinder notes that there is likely little correlation between the educational requirements of a job and the degree to which it can be offshored. But I am surprised that Blinder is not very enthusiastic about encouraging more education. There are many reasons to stress the importance of education, beyond any acquisition of skills that might take place. Individuals with a higher degree of educational attainment fare better in the labor market and are precisely those who are most able to land on their feet after being displaced. In 2005, the unemployment rate was 7.6 percent among those who did not have a high school degree, 4.7 percent among those with a high school degree, 3.9 percent among those with some education beyond high school, and 2.3 percent among those with a bachelor's degree or more (Statistical Abstract 2007, Table 613). My own hunch is that greater education allows people to set their sights beyond their own region of the country and hence have a greater willingness to move long distances to take advantage of new opportunities. (Blanchard and Katz [1992] identify interregional labor mobility as an important source of labor market adjustment in the United States.)

On government-sponsored retraining programs, there are reasons to be skeptical that such public policies can accomplish much. In the 1950s and 1960s, there was a great deal of concern expressed about technological unemployment. In the 1960 election campaign, John F. Kennedy suggested that automation offered "hope of a new prosperity for labor and a new abundance for America," but added that it "carries the dark menace of industrial dislocation, increasing unemployment, and deepening poverty." In February 1962, President Kennedy described worker displacement as "the major domestic challenge, really, of the sixties—to maintain full employment at a time when automation, of course, is replacing men." Secretary of Labor Arthur Goldberg warned that the Second Industrial Revolution would eliminate 1.8 million manufacturing and agricultural positions over the next year alone.

For this reason, the Department of Labor created an Office of Automation and Manpower whose purpose was to anticipate technological change and prepare occupational guidance (Bix 2000, 265–268). I don't know how useful this government office proved to be, but I suspect its contribution to smoothing the transition brought about by structural change was negligible. The resilient and dynamic American economy created such vast opportunities in the 1960s that the Office of Automation and Manpower was a bit player. Looking ahead, do we really expect the federal government to shape America's workforce for the challenges of the twenty-first century?

Let me close with a final observation about economic pessimism.

This is a story from Robert Fogel (2005). Simon Kuznets, who taught economic growth at Harvard, used to say that if you wanted to find accurate forecasts for the future, you shouldn't listen to what the economists said. Economists have been pretty uniformly too pessimistic about our economic prospects. For example, economists at the end of the nineteenth century wrote that progress had been so great over the previous half century that it could not possibly continue, and so forth. According to Kuznets, you would come closest to an accurate forecast if you read writers of science fiction, but even they were too pessimistic. (For example, Jules Verne recognized that we might eventually get to the moon, but he couldn't conceive of the technology that actually made the journey possible.)

An unfortunate example of this is Alvin Hansen, to whom this conference series is dedicated. He devoted his presidential address to the American Economic Association in 1938 to the idea of secular stagnation. The issue was not whether growth in GDP would come to an end, but whether a high level of government spending was necessary to prevent a high level of permanent unemployment, even if GDP did grow. His address triggered a large literature in economics on stagnation and oversaving. These fears were compounded by the worry that the United States would experience massive unemployment after World War II, when twenty-one million people (soldiers and defense industry workers) were thrown into a labor market of about sixty million. These fears were not realized.

I think that Alan Blinder is right in that offshoring will be an important part of the world economy in coming years, but I expect—or at least have some reason for hope—that the transition will be much smoother than he anticipates.

Note

1. According to the article, the rupee has appreciated 9 percent against the dollar from January to May 2007, and "wages have risen as much as 25 percent a year in some sectors, as demand for skilled professionals starts to outstrip supply." Heather Timmons, "Currency's Rise Stokes Concerns in India," *New York Times*, May 24, 2007.

References

Amiti, Mary, and Shang-Jin Wei. 2005. "Fear of Service Outsourcing: Is It Justified?" *Economic Policy* 20, no. 42 (April): 307–347.

Baumol, William J. 2002. *The Free-Market Innovation Machine: Analyzing the Growth Miracle of Capitalism*. Princeton, NJ: Princeton University Press.

Bix, Amy Sue. 2000. *Inventing Ourselves Out of Jobs?: America's Debate over Technological Unemployment, 1929–1981*. Baltimore, MD: Johns Hopkins University Press.

Blanchard, Olivier Jean, and Lawrence F. Katz. 1992. "Regional Evolutions." *Brookings Papers on Economic Activity* 1 (April): 1–75.

Blinder, Alan. 2006. "Offshoring: The Next Industrial Revolution." *Foreign Affairs* 85, no. 2 (March–April): 113–128.

Brown, Clair, John Haltiwanger, and Julia Lane. 2006. *Economic Turbulence: Is a Volatile Economy Good for America?* Chicago: University of Chicago Press.

Fogel, Robert. 2005. "Reconsidering Expectations of Economic Growth after World War II from the Perspective of 2004." NBER Working Paper No. 11125. February.

Irwin, Douglas A. 1996. *Against the Tide: An Intellectual History of Free Trade*. Princeton, NJ: Princeton University Press.

Kirkegaard, Jacob Funk. 2007. "Offshoring, Outsourcing, and Production Relocation—Labor Market Effects in the OECD Countries and Developing Asia." Peter G. Peterson Institute for International Economics, Working Paper 07–2. April.

LORI G. KLETZER

One tradition, for commentators at these events, is to lead with issues and points of common ground. Common ground is an even-handed, even safe, method of providing discussion. There is indeed common ground between Professors Blinder and Bhagwati:

- Validity (benefits) of exploiting comparative advantage
- Modern comparative advantage is "kaleidoscopic," fluid and movable, not anchored in natural resources.
- À la Gomery and Baumol (2000), Samuelson (2004), and others before, the home country can become worse off if the foreign country gets better at producing the good of the home country's comparative advantage.
- We are not talking about a phenomenon that will lead to massive (or mass) unemployment.
- Overall, a defense of free trade

The "debate" is not about these points (at least in my mind). The debate is also not, in my mind, about Alan S. Blinder's "second thoughts about free trade," as recently characterized by David Wessel and Bob Davis (2007). The debate is about the size, scope, and impact of services off-shoring. It seems fair to label Blinder as a "this is somewhat new and a big deal" on this, and Jagdish Bhagwati as a "what's new, not going to be that big" on the question. In other words, a real debate.

The task Blinder has taken on is not as easy one—analyti-cally, methodologically, or in the politics of what we say as economists. What I mean by that is his point is that services offshoring will be *big*, and it will be costly. I'd like to focus my comments on both BIG and on costly, in reverse order.

Because traditionally the gains from "free trade" have played a much larger role in economic discourse than any discussion of the costs, there seems to be some notion of skepticism when influential scholars pick up the refrain that benefits are net, with (often considerable) gross costs. Speak-ing from experience, there is a slightly pariah-like existence for those who discuss costs of globalization. Some see us as just one step away from the abyss of protectionism. I think we've let others define the debate, and frame the responses, by arguing among ourselves. Let me share an example from Blinder's written comments: "If this new wave of international trade (offshoring) is no more than business as usual, then the appropriate policy response is approximately nothing. Laissez-faire will fare just fine; the main trick is to avoid protectionism."

I respectfully disagree—let's take business as usual as "no different from the decades of trade-related manufacturing job loss" (yes—loosely defined, let's not argue about trade vs. technology), then the appropriate policy response is *not to do nothing*. Doing nothing is part of the problem right now. Doing nothing may invite protectionism, and doing something may (at the risk of sounding politically naïve) hold off protectionism. Not having a coherent and holistic treatment (Bhagwati's words), in adjustment assistance programs, creates anxiety, and with the size of the services sector, that's a lot of anxiety and much of it with some political might.

That brings me to size. BIG is one of the real issues confronting us today.

When I was measuring the costs of trade-related job loss, while the label "trade-related" was provocative, I could always hide behind the knowledge that the numbers were relatively small (on the order of 250,000–300,000 workers per year). The labor market costs were considerable, as scaled up by Bradford, Grieco, and Hufbauer (2005) and coauthors, about $54 billion in lifetime earnings. There is no such safety in Blinder's remarks: thirty to forty million workers, at risk today, based on current employment, as potentially offshorable (the upper limit). Thirty to forty million is a very big "number," one worth pursuing.

As Blinder acknowledges, this whole enterprise is purely speculative. I got into the question of measuring services trade and the size and scope of offshoring about three years ago, starting with work with Brad Jensen (Jensen and Kletzer 2006), and the data limitations are notable (we are still in the manufacturing era in terms of measuring services trade). These limitations create opportunities for innovative techniques, as Jensen and I explored in trying to measure potentially tradable services.

One aspect of offshoring is the notion that some jobs are movable (jobs that we perhaps didn't think were movable before). The literature on offshoring posits that movable jobs are those with little face-to-face customer contact; with high information content; and whose work process is Internet enabled and/or telecommutable. A great deal of attention is paid to Internet-enabled: the expansion of broadband and wireless (and the broad use of "off the shelf" software programs) having greatly reduced the "transportation costs" of information.

We can find this type of information in O*Net, the successor to the DOT. Information is organized by detailed occupation (at the Standard Occupational Classification level), in a large number of categories (e.g., tasks, tools and technology, work activities, work context, skills, abilities). The category "Tasks" is very occupation-specific and not easily used across detailed occupations. The category "Work Activities" offers detailed information for building measures of offshorability; characteristics such as no face-to-face customer contact, high information processing content, and Internet-enabled.

Blinder focuses on two issues: (1) whether the work can be delivered to a remote location; and (2) whether the job must be performed at a specific (U.S.) location. In his subjective measure, Blinder concentrates on one characteristic of the delivery of services: the separation of customer and supplier that he labels "impersonally-delivered services." Basically, impersonally delivered services can be delivered electronically, incorporating the vast improvement in ICT. His subjective index does not incorporate any attributes related to the kind of work sent down the wire, such as information context or Internet enabling. Most important, in terms of the area of traditional U.S. comparative advantage, Blinder does not consider the creativity or routineness of work. As Bhagwati notes in his remarks, there are many high-skill and high-value (creative) services that, while transmittable electronically, pose opportunities for American workers and firms to penetrate foreign markets.

Bhagwati's comments extend beyond this focus on the cross-border services flows in Blinder to the full range of services supply. Because research in this area must address the dynamic nature of services offshoring, it is necessarily forward-looking. As the production and consumption of services becomes more global, all the various modes of services supply should be considered. Blinder's personally-delivered services are described in WTO (undated) as "the simultaneous physical presence of both producer and consumer." This is possible through cross-border movements of the consumer (mode 2), the establishment of a commercial presence within a market (mode 3), or the temporary movement of the service provider himself (mode 4).[1]

I think an objective ranking is possible; we all would agree that replication requires one, even one with some problems. Let me take a minute to share mine.

Working more broadly with the O*Net Work Activities information, eleven Work Activities measures were used to construct a measure of offshorability.

On information content:
  Getting information (+)
  Processing information (+)
  Analyzing Data or Information (+)
  Documenting/Recording Information (+)
On Internet-enabled:
  Interacting with computers (+)
On face-to-face contact:
  Assisting or Caring for Others (−)
  Performing or Working Directly with the Public (−)
  Establishing or Maintaining Interpersonal Relationships (−)
On the routine or creative nature of work:
  Making Decisions and Solving Problems (−)
  Thinking Creatively (−)
As a proxy for the "on-site" nature of work:
  Inspecting equipment, structures or material (−)

For now, I'll skip the details of my index (interested readers are directed to Jensen and Kletzer 2007). I think of the index as ordinal, paying no attention to distance between occupations.

Here are the most offshorable, and the least offshorable.

The top 20 most offshorable:

		Employment	Median earnings
1	Mathematical Technicians	1,430	$36,470
2	Biochemists and Biophysicists	17,690	$71,000
3	Statisticians	17,480	$62,450
4	Title Examiners, Abstractors, and Searchers	64,580	$35,120
5	Credit Authorizers, Checkers, and Clerks	65,410	$29,330
6	Weighers, Measurers, Checkers, and Samplers, Recordkeeping	79,050	$25,310
7	Data Entry Keyers	296,700	$23,810
8	Accountants and Auditors	1,051,220	$52,210

9	Medical Transcriptionists	90,380	$29,080
10	Actuaries	15,770	$81,640
11	Market Research Analysts	195,710	$57,300
12	Astronomers	970	$104,670
13	Bookkeeping, Accounting, and Auditing Clerks	1,815,340	$29,490
14	Mechanical Drafters	74,650	$43,350
15	Economists	12,470	$73,690
16	Mathematicians	2,930	$80,920
17	Sociologists	3,500	$52,760
18	OperationsResearchAnalysts	52,530	$62,180
19	Survey Researchers	21,650	$31,140
20	Credit Analysts	61,500	$50,370

The bottom 20, or the least offshorable:

		Employment	Median earnings
438	Bartenders	480,010	$15,850
439	Craft Artists	4,300	$22,430
440	Lifeguards, Ski Patrol, and Other Recreational Protective Service Workers	107,620	$16,910
441	Dancers	16,240	*
442	Choreographers	16,150	$32,950
443	Animal Trainers	8,320	$24,800
444	Self-Enrichment Education Teachers	141,650	$32,360
445	Child Care Workers	557,680	$17,050
446	Models	1,430	$22,700
447	Preschool Teachers, Except Special Education	348,690	$21,990

448	Fitness Trainers and Aerobics Instructors	189,220	$25,840
449	Surgical Technologists	83,680	$34,830
450	Crossing Guards	69,390	$20,050
451	Massage Therapists	37,670	$32,890
452	Gaming Dealers	82,320	$14,260
453	Actors	59,590	*
454	Manicurists and Pedicurists	42,960	$18,280
455	Hairdressers, Hairstylists, and Cosmetologists	338,910	$20,610
456	Flight Attendants	99,590	$46,680
457	Barbers	13,630	$21,760

*not available

How many? I'm not very comfortable right now drawing a line. If I had to draw one line, my estimates suggest thirty-eight million potentially offshorable jobs; fifty-five million not (below the line).

I find some link between potential offshorability and educational attainment. The O*Net data offer information on educational attainment, based on BLS data on fractions of jobholders with varying levels of education. Focusing on fraction with at least a BA degree, the rank correlation between educational attainment and relative offshorability is +0.306—occupations with a greater share of BA holders are more highly ranked as offshorable. The top quartile of jobs in the ranking has a mean percentage of BA+ degree holders of 61 percent; the second quartile, 53.7 percent; the third quartile 47.3 percent; and the bottom quartile, 29.1 percent. The least offshorable jobs are the least formally educated and have lower median annual earnings.

One of the next steps will be to refine our estimates, within occupations. Not all jobs in an occupation will be offshored.

Perhaps there will be variation by firm size and industry (some industries being more tradable than others).

So, it is likely that many service workers will have to join manufacturing's production workers in learning to live with job insecurity. And we have to start measuring their costs of adjustment.

How soon? We don't really know. We do know that advancing technology will continue to increase the feasibility of providing services from remote locations. For now and perhaps the foreseeable future, however, most high-value work will require creative interaction among employees, interaction that is facilitated by physical proximity and personal contact. Moreover, in many fields, closeness to customers and knowledge of local conditions are also of great importance.

I can't possibly disagree with the proposed remedies:

Expand TAA to include services workers (Not easy operationally—how to measure trade)?

Expand TAA to all displaced workers

Reform UI

Expand EITC

Portable health insurance and pensions

Wage-loss insurance

Educational system (not a panacea and will require much thought)

These are important details that require a coherent approach. On that I think we can all agree.

Note

1. As Bhagwati notes, Sampson and Snape 1985 is an early and influential contribution to understanding trade in services.

References

Bradford, Scott C., Paul L.E. Grieco, and Gary Clyde Hufbauer. 2005. "The Payoff to America from Global Integration," in C. Fred Bergsten and the Institute for International Economics, *The United States and the World Economy: Foreign Economic Policy for the Next Decade*, 65–101. Washington, DC: Institute for International Economics.

Gomory, Ralph E., and William J. Baumol. 2000. *Global Trade and Conflicting National Interest*. Cambridge, MA: MIT Press.

Jensen, J. Bradford, and Lori G. Kletzer. 2006. "Tradable Services: Understanding the Scope and Impact of Services Offshoring," in Susan M. Collins and Lael Brainard, eds., *Brookings Trade Forum 2005: Offshoring White-Collar Work*, 75–134. Washington, DC: Brookings Institution.

Jensen, J. Bradford, and Lori G. Kletzer. 2007. "The Scope of Tradable Services and the Task Content of Offshorable Services Jobs." Unpublished manuscript. May.

Sampson, Gary P., and Richard H. Snape. 1985. "Identifying the Issues in Trade in Services." *The World Economy* 8, no. 2: 171–182.

Samuelson, Paul A. 2004. "Where Ricardo and Mill Rebut and Confirm Arguments of Mainstream Economists against Globalization." *Journal of Economic Perspectives* 18, no. 3 (Summer): 135–146.

Wessel, David, and Bob Davis. 2007. "Pain from Free Trade Spurs Second Thoughts." *Wall Street Journal*, March 30, A1.

World Trade Organization. n.d. "The General Agreement on Trade in Services (GATS): Objectives, Coverage and Disciplines." http://www.wto.org/english/tratop_e/serv_e/gatsqa_e.htm#3.

ROBERT Z. LAWRENCE

In his superbly written chapter, Alan S. Blinder assumes the role of Paul Revere riding in to warn us of impending doom. It is not the British who are coming, he tells us, it is the Indians. Electronic off-shoring, he warns, is going to be "a big deal." Though on balance the economy will benefit, there is also going to be massive disruption that we need to prepare for. According to Blinder, unemployment (frictional, structural, and Keynesian) is bound to rise, real wages and the real exchange rate are bound to fall, and the United States is bound to become more protectionist. Unlike Paul Revere, instead of seeking to mobilize resistance to these invaders, Blinder advises U.S. workers to head for hills and escape the Indian hoards: he argues they should all be trained for the safer jobs that produce personal services.

But is Blinder Paul Revere or just Chicken Little? Is he not warning us that the sky is falling when in fact there is little reason to panic? I believe that he is excessively pessimistic and, precisely because his paper is superficially persuasive, I am concerned that he could engender unnecessary alarm and provoke the very protectionist responses that he says he'd like to avoid.

And this subject does scare people. In his compelling contribution to this collection, Jagdish Bhagwati traces the receptivity of the media to any evidence that economists may be rethinking their views on the benefits of trade. Many Americans do not understand that our high living standards basically reflect our high productivity levels, and they find it quite plausible that, in an integrated world economy, our incomes could fall to Indian levels. We've already seen how easily the public can be panicked when claims were made in 2003–2004 that Indian offshoring was the most important reason for slow U.S. employment growth. As is widely acknowledged now, the scale of that offshoring was far too small to have been significant, but nonetheless a few anecdotes were widely taken as representative of broader trends.[1] Blinder seeks to warn us that next time could be different, and many of the same people are bound to take him seriously.

In my view, Blinder is correct when he says that the changes from offshoring could be a big deal and the potential benefits could be large. We know that the gains from trade are directly related to the price differences that exist before trade occurs and international wage differences are generally much larger than international price differences. I also agree with Blinder that policies should avoid trade protection, seek to compensate the losers, and do more to facilitate adjustment, training, and education. But none of these policy prescriptions really hinge on this debate.

I do however have four basic disagreements with Blinder that I will now elaborate upon. I believe that the adjustments will be less disruptive than Blinder suggests because they will be spread out over a long time; I find his claim that the threat of offshoring has already depressed wages unconvincing; I believe that the one piece of novel policy advice he gives—that American workers should be trained for high-end personal service jobs—is seriously misguided, and I think that the protectionist pressures are likely to be less than he fears.

Massive disruption? Blinder undertakes an interesting exercise that classifies jobs according to the degree to which they could be offshored. His midrange estimate is that these account for 26 percent of current U.S. employment. If he is correct, this is reason for comfort rather than alarm. As Blinder admits, this number is an *upper bound* estimate because it reflects jobs that are "potentially" offshorable because of the characteristics of the tasks they entail, but it ignores many other considerations that could make it uneconomic or impractical to do so.

If Blinder is correct, rather than going into new unchartered waters as it undergoes this offshoring adjustment, the U.S. labor market would be returning to a level of international exposure we are already familiar with. In 1970, for example, the share of Americans employed in manufacturing, mining, and agriculture was 26 percent—the same share that could be exposed according to Blinder's estimate of potential offshorability. As this number reminds us, given manufacturing's shrinking employment share, there is a powerful force operating to reduce trade exposure in the opposite direction and continuously removing a substantial share of employment from tradability. If this latter trend continues over the next few decades, while the services share will rise, the aggregate amount of exposure could therefore be significantly less than 26 percent.

Moreover, about half of Blinder's number includes jobs that have already been potentially offshorable for a long time—namely, those in manufacturing and some services. Indeed, *currently* 12 percent of Americans work in sectors producing tradable goods—namely, manufacturing, mining, and agriculture—and U.S. services exports and imports amount to another 3 percent of GDP, so in fact Blinder is implicitly telling us that the challenge facing the United States is an increase in the share of potentially tradable jobs in total employment by something on the order of 10 percent over a period of two to three decades. Even if every one of these jobs had to be replaced by another, on average the turnover would average less than a half a percent *per year*. Yet we know that in the United States labor turnover is currently on the order of 3 percent *per month*, so it's unconvincing to argue, as Blinder does, that this effect is likely to have a significant impact on the total amount of churning in the labor market and/or on the level of structural and Keynesian unemployment. I would acknowledge that all job loss is not created equal, and for some people the adjustment could be particularly painful if offshoring requires people to change occupations rather than just change jobs. But I am unconvinced that the scale and pain is going to be greater than we are already familiar with.

A crucial question is how quickly these changes are likely to occur, and my answer based on the evidence from the goods market is that change will come slowly. Tom Friedman notwithstanding, an overwhelming amount of empirical evidence indicates that the world is actually very round (and bumpy).[2] To be sure trade *is* affected by relative prices and costs, but borders continue to matter a lot and adjustments across borders are very slow. The full effects of exchange rates on trade flows, for example, can take up to five years. The many gravity models that have been estimated confirm that distance is important and by an amount that is much greater than can be ascribed to transportation costs. Similarly, detailed comparisons of price differentials in Bradford and Lawrence 2004, for example, show that absolute price differences of similar goods have averaged 20 percent between the United States and Canada, thirty percent between the United States and Europe, and 50 percent between the United States and Japan, and yet still are not arbitraged away. Why? Even when communication and transportation costs are zero, a large number of obstacles and inhibitions remain: these include differences in laws, culture, language, policies, regulations, and standards. Moreover, it's not enough just to know that a service can be obtained more cheaply. Particularly for complex transactions that require depending on foreign suppliers for key inputs, old relationships must be broken and new ones established. And building the necessary trust will require time and favorable experiences. And on the supply side, Indians and others have to build up their capacity and skills and establish their reputations. The implication is that on both the demand and supply sides, adjustments are bound to be protracted.

Depressed wages? Blinder presents us with a regression that he claims shows that the mere threat of future offshoring has already depressed the wages of occupations that are most susceptible to offshoring by 14 percent. But the regression is not credible and certainly should not be given this interpretation. First, the coefficient is far too large. The studies of the impact of trade on the relative wages of unskilled U.S. workers with the largest estimates indicate effects of at most 6 percent.[3] Similarly, the premiums commanded by workers who unionize are on the order of 15 percent. It is unlikely that the mere threat of outsourcing in the future would be of the same order of magnitude as actually organizing and bargaining for higher wages. Second, the cross-section regression that Blinder uses is the wrong specification for testing his claim. He uses only observations from 2004, but we need observations from years before offshoring was feasible to test his claim properly. And third, the equation controls only for education, but other attributes of both the jobs and the workers could bias the coefficient on the offshoring variable downward. For example, it is plausible that the most offshorable jobs are more routine, are less skilled, and have higher turnover—all of which could account for the effect he finds.

Actually, it is interesting that Blinder finds a negative and statistically significant coefficient on only the occupations that are the most offshorable. This suggests that if it does advance, offshoring might cause some dislocation but not increase inequality. I think this is an example of the larger paradox that the more globalization advances, the less inequality it is likely to cause. Initially, only low-wage workers will experience adverse competitive effects, but as more of the economy is subject to competitive pressure, relatively more skilled workers will also experience these effects.

Other harm? I also have problems with Blinder's prediction that the U.S. real exchange rate is likely to decline and reduce our living standards. It is certainly possible that if foreigners are able to compete in the services the United States currently *exports*, our terms of trade could decline. But if offshoring is indeed a "big deal," many services currently not traded will be imported and exported. This is akin to opening up a country to trade, and there is a strong presumption the impact on living standards will be beneficial.

Get out of the way? Although he pays lip service to the additional exports that are going to be generated, Blinder seems to forget about export jobs when he advises workers to get trained for non-offshorable jobs. If the United States does import large amounts of services, it will eventually have to pay for these by producing more tradable goods and services at home. And ironically, the weaker the real exchange rate, the more plentiful such jobs are going to be. This means that advice to get out of the tradable sector may be quite wrong. Moreover, if jobs in impersonal services do become riskier, employers are likely eventually to have to compensate those who take them with higher wages. Indeed, Jensen and Kletzer (2005) find that service jobs that are tradable domestically pay significantly higher wages.[4] Their evidence not only contradicts Blinder's wage regression but implies that workers who ignore his advice could earn more than those who do not. Finally, I would go back to Blinder's own estimate. If 26 percent of all jobs are potentially offshorable, this implies 74 percent are *not* even potentially offshorable. This means that the picture of workers all being crowded into a small part of the economy is not really accurate.

Protectionism? Finally, the politics. I would not rule out the possibility that protectionist pressures could increase if the U.S. labor market fails to provide adequate employment opportunities and rising wages. As the experience in 2004 indicates, international trade often makes a convenient scapegoat. I would agree that some more educated workers could be mobilized in this direction by the experience of international competition. But there are also several factors associated with offshoring that make it *less* likely to give rise to the protectionism associated with trade in goods.

First, whereas the primary beneficiaries from imports of finished goods are consumers, who are poorly organized, the beneficiaries of offshored services are U.S. firms that can act collectively.

Second, usually, when we consider the politics of protection, the expectation is that inter-industry trade is likely to be more disruptive than intra-industry trade. In addition, we would expect owners and workers from the same import competing industry to oppose liberalization because both experience erosion in the returns to their specific factors of production. But offshoring involves intra-firm trade, and some workers and owners within the very same firm are likely to gain from outsourcing, so again effective opposition is likely to be more difficult to mobilize.

Third, there are unlikely to be large layoffs in individual large unionized plants like steel or automobiles. The employment impact of imports could be felt within firms that are otherwise able to operate and indeed may well become more profitable.

Fourth, the dislocation is likely to be quite diffuse, rather than concentrated geographically within a particular region that makes industries like textiles more likely to exert protectionist pressures.

And finally, it is actually very difficult to protect against this trade since, as Barry Eichengreen has observed, it "comes in through the Windows." Multinational firms are a large part of the U.S. economy, and it is very difficult to stop many operations from being performed abroad. The major protectionist instrument available to those seeking to curtail offshoring to India is through discriminatory government procurement. But this does not capture most of the potential activity.

In sum, I am actually somewhat calmer about offshoring than I was before I read this chapter, because my priors were that a much higher share of services was potentially offshorable. I conclude that services liberalization presents both the developed and developing countries with exciting new opportunities to benefit from trade. A flexible U.S. economy, aided by the right safety net and redistribution policies, should be able to take advantage of these opportunities as long as the change is relatively gradual.

Notes

1. See National Academy of Administration (2006a, b), Amiti and Wei (2005), and International Monetary Fund (2007), all of whom find that while it has grown in recent years, the offshoring of services remains very limited.

2. For a superb and entertaining review of Friedman's book that makes similar points, see Leamer 2007.

3. Cline 1997 has a good summary.

4. Jensen and Kletzer 2005.

References

Amiti, Mary, and Shang-Jin Wei. 2005. "Fear of Service Outsourcing: Is it Justified?" *Economic Policy* 20 (April): 308–347.

Bradford, Scott C., and Robert Z. Lawrence. 2004. *Has Globalization Gone Far Enough? The Costs of Fragmented Markets.* Washington, DC: Institute for International Economics.

Cline, William R. 1997. *Trade and Income Distribution.* Washington, DC: Institute for International Economics.

International Monetary Fund. 2007. "The Globalization of Labor." In *World Economic Outlook: Spillovers and Cycles in the Global Economy.* Washington, DC: International Monetary Fund.

Jensen, J. Bradford, and Lori G. Kletzer. 2005. "Tradable Services: Understanding the Scope and Impact of Services Outsourcing." Working Paper No. 05–9. Washington, DC: Institute for International Economics.

Leamer, Edward E. 2007. "A Flat World, a Level Playing Field, a Small World After All, or None of the Above? A Review of Thomas L. Friedman's *The World Is Flat." Journal of Economic Literature* 45, no. 1 (March): 83–126.

National Academy of Public Administration. 2006a. "Off-Shoring: An Elusive Phenomenon." Academy Project no. 2051–000. Washington, DC: National Academy of Public Administration. January.

National Academy of Public Administration. 2006b. "Off-Shoring: How Big is IT?" Academy Project no. 2051–000. Washington, DC: National Academy of Public Administration. October.

4   Responses

JAGDISH BHAGWATI

I plan to be brief since the long afterword to my newly issued
In Defense of Globalization (New York: Oxford University
Press) contains many arguments that effectively respond to,
or anticipate, much of what is said by Alan S. Blinder and
by the discussants. Besides, many additional arguments are
contained in the book that I am just finishing, titled *Terrified
by Trade: The Paradox of Protectionism in the United States* (New
York: Oxford University Press), slated to be published in late
2009 to catch the attention of the new U.S. administration.[1]

The Fragility of Long-Term Forecasts

First, I daresay, no one can foretell what will happen down
the road, as we extend our gaze way beyond the horizon. A
cataclysm? Gradual change? The classical economists predicted the arrival of the stationary state, believe it or not.
Marx predicted the immiseration of the proletariat as capitalism unfolded, but history took him by surprise.

In the 1950s, as the new nations arrived from colonization
to independence, virtually every developmental economist

predicted that the two sleeping giants, China and India, would awaken. But, largely thanks to bad economic policies —in China's case, imposed by communist politics; in India's case, by knee-jerk-interventionism economics and virtual autarky at the margin—these giants continued to snore for almost four decades, while the small and insignificant nations of the Far East—South Korea, Taiwan, Singapore, and Hong Kong—raced ahead, for reasons that have much to do with their export orientation. This led to a high marginal efficiency of capital and high productive investment rates that, in turn, meant that the rapidly rising exports were accompanied by imports of cheap late-but-not-latest-vintage capital goods whose prices were low but whose productivity was high because of a highly literate labor force due to phenomenally high literacy rates exceeding 90 percent.[2]

Finally, these giants have woken up and are growing at accelerated rates, causing the mistakenly exaggerated negative views of our economic prospects and also our workers' and middle class professionals' wages and salaries: a matter to which I will address some critical remarks in this response.

But let me ask again: Can we extrapolate these high growth rates, and assume that the two economies will grow at the same high rates for the next three decades, leave aside the even longer time horizon that Blinder perhaps seems to entertain? There are many serious China experts who fear that China faces a real dilemma because its rapid growth, without democracy, has given rise to major impediments to the country's continued growth. Thus, take environment. Without the countervailing power provided by NGOs, opposition parties, an independent judiciary, and a free press, environmental degradation can get out of hand, as it has. So, the past growth is seriously overestimated, and future growth is compromised. Then again, the rapid growth has created a middle class that is likely to demand more political participation; but an authoritarian system may well react by tightening the regime, creating massive disruptions, rather than by accommodating these demands. In short, continued high growth rates in China over the long haul are not certain.[3]

So, I am not sure at all that Blinder's desire to look far into the future, and his tendency to say that whatever I say to contradict his dire predictions in his *Foreign Affairs* article will not hold at some distant date, is terribly convincing. Maybe he will turn out to be right, perhaps for the wrong reason; but at seventy-three years old, I am unlikely to live long enough to rue my skepticism.

Linking Globalization to Stagnation of Wages

Richard Freeman makes a brave attempt at saying that trade is indeed increasing pressure on wages, so let me say some more on this question. An early paper of his with Larry Katz and George Borjas used the "factor content" approach to argue that both trade and immigration were harming wages and by how much. I challenged the methodology at the time and the issue was then the subject of a set of essays by leading trade scholars in 2000 in the *Journal of International Economics*, where it became clear that extremely restrictive assumptions, going well beyond those customarily made, had to be used to make the inferences that these authors were making.[4]

Then again many empirical studies until the 1990s, by Paul Krugman, Robert Lawrence and others, argued that the effect of trade with poor countries on real wages of the unskilled in the rich countries was, at best, limited. My own work, in a 1999 paper titled "Play It Again Sam: A New Look at Trade and Wages," in the T. N. Srinivasan fest-schrift, argued that the effect of accumulation and technical change in the rapidly growing countries of East Asia had been to raise, not lower, the relative prices of labor-intensive goods during the years when real wages were stagnant and therefore the Stolper-Samuelson theorem would have worked to moderate (not accentuate) the decline in wages coming from labor-saving technical change.[5]

Now, Paul Krugman, in the two columns in the *New York Times* that I referred to in chapter 1, has weighed in on the side of the Democratic candidates who are captive to the unions who are pushing the proposition that trade with the poor countries is undermining our workers' wages, by writing that "there's growing concern in this country about the effects of globalization on wages, largely because imports of manufactured goods from low-wage countries have surged, doubling as a share of GDP since 1993."[6] Indeed, he wrote about how the increasing share of U.S. imports from developing countries to 6 percent "may" have changed the situation from the time when he wrote opposing the link:

Still, when the effects of third-world exports on U.S. wages first became an issue in the 1990s, a number of economists—myself included—looked at the data and concluded that any negative effects on U.S. wages were modest. The trouble now is that these effects may no longer be as modest as they were, because imports of manufactured goods from the third world have grown dramatically—from just 2.5 percent of GDP in 1990 to 6 percent in 2006.[7]

But of course we need to look directly at goods prices to infer factor prices and real wages (as I did in my 1999 paper, just cited), so his argument seems to be incomplete, even mistaken. Besides, consider that non-farm employment in the United States is 138 million. Of this, only 16.3 percent are employed in goods—that is, manufacturing. These goods include a number of skill-intensive items like aircraft, computers, and sophisticated machinery. So, in the end, only a terribly small proportion of the labor force is competing with labor-intensive imports from the developing countries. Besides, many of the imports from developing countries are from fairly developed countries like South Korea, Taiwan, and Singapore who are now exporting skill-intensive manufactures. Besides, Krugman ignores the extremely important fact that the manufacture of many labor-intensive goods has now been abandoned in the United States so that any decline in their world prices would only help labor by cheapening consumption. Therefore, unless Krugman produces evidence to substantiate his assertion, it is not possible to take it seriously.[8]

In fact, in his splendid monograph on "Blue Collar Blues: Is Trade to Blame for Rising U.S. Income Inequality?" (February 2008, Peterson Institute for International Economics, Washington, DC), based on the paper I cited in chapter 1, Robert Lawrence has demonstrated definitively that trade does not stand up as a villain in the story of increasing wage inequality. Nor, for that matter, can it be argued to explain stagnation in real wages of the unskilled. I would say not that the jury is out, but that it has come in and the verdict is an acquittal.

The Media et al.

Freeman also raises his eyebrows, ever so mildly, at my "quips" and my arguing that the media have hyped up the loss of consensus on free trade among economists. Well, quips, or rather bon mots and wit, can convey an esoteric point from economics much more effectively than technicalities. I daresay that this ensures that many more of my target audience read what I write; I recommend the technique to him.

When I say that the media have repeatedly indulged in hype on this issue, I do give chapter and verse to defend what I say. Aside from the fact that there is no story in saying that economists continue to be in agreement on the merits of free trade, and even a promotion if you say instead that the consensus has disappeared, I do think that the United States reporting on economics (with some superb exceptions like Peter Passell and Michael Weinstein, formerly of the *New York Times*, who had degrees in Economics from MIT and Yale and held prestigious academic positions before they turned into full-time journalists) is generally well below the level you find in England—the best economics is written by journalists in the *Financial Times* and the *Economist*, where world-class columnists such as Martin Wolf and Clive Crook are First Class graduates of Oxbridge —and in Germany where Ph.D.s do the economics writing. The products of even our best schools of journalism traditionally come from English literature and are taught how to write, not what to write. Given this situation, I was one of the founders of the media specialization several years ago in the School for International Affairs at Columbia. Our students had 101 in economics, international law, political science, and international relations; and they had one regional specialization like Russia or East Asia. I and James Chace, the distinguished former editor of *Foreign Affairs* and an accomplished writer, taught the students how to write economics op-eds. Our graduates turned out to be so good that they were hired in preference over the graduates of the world-renowned Columbia School of Journalism! Today, of course, the journalism school has wound up embracing the model we had pioneered, with Nicholas Lemann appointed dean to develop his school in exactly the direction that I and Chace had pioneered.

But what is perhaps surprising is the way in which this media hype has been compounded by the media's inability to respond to politicians' witting and unwitting errors that feed unjustified protectionism today. I wonder how many scholars among us noticed that when Hillary Clinton badly misquoted Paul Samuelson to justify her "pause" on trade and her triangulation or prevarications on trade liberalization, the only major newspaper that took up the issue and condemned her was the *Financial Times*, a foreign newspaper!

Since protectionism is today an affliction of the Democrats in particular, and partisanship in politics is intense since the Republicans are fearful of losing power and Democrats are salivating at the prospect of seizing it, a small set of key economists among the Democrats have naturally turned to ambivalence on the issue, saying that the labor opponents of freer trade "have a point." This "prudential" behavior by economists active in politics, and agitated by the Bush administration's dismal performance overall, is understandable. But I am certain that ultimately good sense and good economics will prevail.

Notes

1. This book will deal with witting protectionism that comes from protectionists, examining why some of the lobbies like AFL-CIO are terrified by trade and seek to undermine trade deals or to burden them with de facto protectionist provisions such as labor standards requirements aimed at raising the cost of production by rivals abroad closer on these dimensions

to their own. On the other hand, we also are witness to the unwitting wounds inflicted on multilateral free trade by free traders who mistakenly pursue Preferential Trade Agreements (PTAs), such as the proliferating Free Trade Agreements (FTAs). To address these issues, I have written a companion volume titled *Termites in the Trading System: How Preferential Agreements are Undermining Free Trade* (New York: Oxford University Press, 2008).

2. I have developed a full explanation of the East Asian miracle along these lines in "The 'Miracle' that Did Happen: Understanding East Asia in Comparative Perspective," reprinted as chapter 4 in my collected essays, *The Wind of the Hundred Days: How Washington Mismanaged Globalization* (Cambridge, MA: MIT Press: 2002).

3. I have developed these arguments in a review of Will Hutton's recent book on China in the *New York Times Book Review* last year (February 18, 2007). For India, and the nature of its reforms and why they and India's democracy promise steady and sustained growth, see my panel remarks in Jagdish Bhagwati and Charles Calomiris, ed., *Sustaining India's Miracle* (New York: Columbia University Press: 2008).

4. See, in particular, Arvind Panagariya's brilliant contribution to the symposium that illuminates the crippling limitations of the factor-content approach. Cf. "Evaluating the Factor-Content Approach to Measuring the Effect of Trade on Wage Inequality," (*Journal of International Economics* 50, no. 1: 91–116). The focus in this paper, as in the other papers in the same issue, is on wage inequality rather than on absolute real wages (the latter requiring added restrictions).

5. The paper has been reprinted as chapter 11 in *The Wind of the Hundred Days*, op. cit.

6. From Paul Krugman's January 4, 2008, *New York Times* op-ed "Dealing with the Dragon."

7. From Paul Krugman's December 28, 2007, *New York Times* op-ed "Trouble with Trade."

8. I suspect that he is also remiss in not distinguishing sharply between the ratio of skilled to unskilled wages and real wages of the unskilled. If wages of the skilled rise more than the wages of the unskilled, the ratio will rise, showing increased inequality so defined; but real wages of the unskilled, which we are trying to explain, will have increased, not fallen. The important work, reported by Robert Feenstra and Gordon Hanson in "Productivity Measurement and the Impact of

Trade and Technology on Wages: Estimates for the U.S., 1972–1990," *Quarterly Journal of Economics* 114 (1999): 907–940, on outsourcing, defined more generally than simply outsourcing of services à la mode 1, shows that while this has led to increased inequality, it has also led to increased real wages of the unskilled. See the discussion of this work in my book *In Defense of Globalization* (New York: Oxford University Press, 2004), 126.

ALAN S. BLINDER

Response to Bhagwati

I take pains to point out in my chapter (and in my other writings) that the issue under debate is *not* whether free trade is a good thing, but rather whether the transition to more offshoring of service jobs will be massive, lengthy, and disruptive.[1] Richard B. Freeman and Lori G. Kletzer take my side in this debate; we all agree that there is something unusual going on, and that it is worth worrying about. Douglas A. Irwin and Robert Z. Lawrence join Jagdish Bhagwati in being more relaxed. Unfortunately, Bhagwati's chapter more or less ignores this entire question in favor of one that is apparently more to his liking: will Blinder's "attack" on free trade endure, or will it wither on the vine like previous waves of "attacks?" So let me address this mythical issue first, and then return to the real one.

According to Bhagwati, I am now one of "the few economists" currently "arrayed against" free trade. Well, that comes as quite a shock to me—and it is flatly contradicted by the opening pages of my chapter. I started the chapter by stating unequivocally that I am not in any sense hostile to trade. Specifically, I wrote early on that "I yield to no one in my defense of free trade" (p. 25). Isn't that clear enough?

Two aspects of Bhagwati's critique strike me as somewhat Marxian—one associated with Karl, the other with Groucho. Let's start with Groucho.

When I peruse the list of other economists who have allegedly tried, but failed, to sack the free trade temple, I feel as if I am being praised by faint damnation. Like Groucho Marx, I'm pretty flattered (and a bit flabbergasted) to be admitted to any club that has Paul Samuelson as a member— except, perhaps, the Belmont Tennis Club. Add Will Baumol, Ralph Gomory, Paul Krugman, and Laura Tyson to the membership rolls, and I'm clamoring for admission. But do any of us deserve our membership cards? Speaking for myself, I'm an unabashed advocate of free trade; and I suspect (or know) that the other alleged members are, too. So, if Bhagwati's question is "Will the Blinder-led assault on free trade succeed or fail?," let me answer it right now: the "assault" will not be "led" and has already failed by default, because it was never attempted and never will be.

Actually, Bhagwati's argument, in common with some remarks by Irwin and Lawrence, is slightly more indirect. It's apparently not so much that *I* am a protectionist, it's that my words can be (and have been) *misconstrued* in ways that have given aid and comfort to the enemies of free trade. According to Irwin (p. 72), I have "resurrected Perot-esque fear about offshoring and India."[2] According to Bhagwati (p. 10), I have been "turned into a new icon for the protectionists even though Blinder always said that he was still a free trader."

Well, I am a free trader. But having been a (very) minor public figure for some time now, I understand that no one can prevent his words from being misconstrued now and then in the media and by politicians—whether deliberately or accidentally. That said, I have learned something from the reactions of many of my fellow economists since I first began to talk and write about offshoring. It is this: because free trade is probably the policy issue that comes closest to getting unanimous support from economists, any economist who utters *any* qualifications or second thoughts that *might possibly* provide ammunition for protectionists is presumed guilty of apostasy. And I mean the analogy literally. It's like deviating from high church dogma—and the thought police are on patrol.

I have two reactions to the quasi-religious fervor. First, free trade fundamentalism advances a pretty odd version of what it means to belong to the established church. I have taught Economics 101 at Princeton University, a bastion of the establishment, for about three decades now. One privilege this job gives me is that of introducing young minds to the principle of comparative advantage and the basic arguments in favor of free trade (and against protectionism)—which I do faithfully and with relish.

When I reach this topic in the course, the first thing I teach students is how and why exploiting comparative advantage leads to gains from trade. And the second thing I teach them is that trade liberalizations normally create both winners and losers.[3] This second lesson hardly originates with me. Don't students at Columbia University learn it, too? After all, as Kletzer notes in her comments, trade openings are *not* Pareto moves. Under what strange version of the catechism does teaching that trade (or change more generally) creates both winners and losers constitute apostasy?

And by the way, I do *not* teach my introductory students that nations might actually be *harmed* by trade, even though that is the clear implication of some classic work by Bhagwati (1968), recently remembered by Samuelson (2004). My attitude is that freshmen should master the basics first;

the qualifications can wait for a subsequent course in trade theory. That said, Bhagwati's theoretical point *is* relevant to the debate over electronic offshoring that we are having in this book. The opening of trade in (heretofore untradable) impersonal services with India and other countries might indeed make the United States as a whole worse off. That's a fact, and we might as well get ready to deal with it, recognizing as we do that protectionism is *not* part of the solution.

My second reaction to the religious approach to free trade brings me to Karl Marx, rather than Groucho. One of the central tenets of Marxism—its macroeconomic component—was that capitalism is subject to the scourge of ever-increasing business cycles. During the Great Depression, that critique struck a little too close to home, and socialism was on the march worldwide. Then John Maynard Keynes figured out a way to ameliorate business cycles within an entirely capitalistic framework. Given the temper of the time, I think it is no exaggeration to say that Keynesianism helped save capitalism from its own excesses. Yet what happened? Keynes's ideas were greeted on the right as apostasy, even as backdoor socialism, for decades; indeed, one occasionally hears quaint vestiges of that attitude even today. Similarly, I believe (as do Freeman and Kletzer) that free trade will be under increasing threat unless we cope better with the coming transition to service offshoring.

One of the reasons to worry is Bhagwati's assertion that "what you 'consume,' in a broad sense, is likely to be far more important to you and to your society's well-being than what you produce" (p. 5). Almost all economists, including me, think this way. Unfortunately for us, almost no one else on earth does. To the vast majority of humankind, earning a decent living is overwhelmingly more important than being able to pick up bargains at Wal-Mart. Our job as economists is to convince the body politic that, once you add up all these Wal-Mart savings, and factor in the new jobs that trade create, the nation is indeed better off. Unfortunately, we have largely failed in this task for over two hundred years.

The application to offshoring is immediate: if Americans come to believe that service offshoring will "destroy" millions of American jobs, even though it reduces costs for many American businesses, support for the open trading system will be difficult to sustain. That is one of the things we worrywarts fret about.

One final, slightly technical, point on Bhagwati's critique needs to be made. He seems irritated that I concentrate on "mode 1" trade in services (e.g., online transmission), to the near exclusion of other modes of service trade. But I did this deliberately and for good reasons. First and foremost, electronic trade is the New New Thing that is likely to grow enormously in years to come. Tourism is old hat. Second, while it is true that "doctors can go to patients, and patients to doctors" (Bhagwati, p. 11), physical movement of either producers or consumers is vastly more costly and time-consuming than movement of electrons. Because of that, it faces some natural limits. But as technology enables trade in an increasing array of services to take place electronically, rather than face-to-face, the natural impediments to trade (e.g., shipping costs, time, . . .) start to melt away. Thus, I strenuously disagree that I was wrong to concentrate on mode 1. Instead, my Paul Revere role is to get people—especially economists, it appears—thinking about mode 1 much more.

Response to Irwin and Lawrence

Both Douglas A. Irwin and Robert Z. Lawrence, in somewhat different ways, make a telling and legitimate point. I
claim that the impending transition to service offshoring
will be both extensive and long-lasting. But the latter implies
that the changes will come gradually. As Irwin and Lawrence correctly point out, gradual adjustments are less disruptive than rapid ones. And they both observe that the
volume of job change that I anticipate is small relative to the
normal job churn in the highly fluid U.S. labor market. I
accept these points as meaningful qualifications to my warn-
ings about how difficult the coming transition is likely to be.
But I repeat, yet again, that I am not a doomsayer. Irwin, for
example, quotes (but then ignores) the clear and unequivo-
cal statement in my 2006 *Foreign Affairs* piece (repeated in
different words many times) that "we should not view the
coming wave of offshoring as an impending catastrophe."
We shouldn't, and I don't.

Lawrence notes that my intermediate guesstimate of
the share of jobs that will eventually become tradable
(roughly 26 percent) is strikingly similar to the number
of jobs that were in the tradable sector in 1970—prior to
most of the shrinkage of the U.S. manufacturing sector
(which is now down to about 10 percent of the workforce).
As he puts it (pp. 93–94), "the U.S. labor market would be
returning to a level of international exposure we are already
familiar with."

This is another good point, and I cannot disagree with it.
But while nothing calamitous has happened during the
(ongoing) transition to a smaller manufacturing sector, I
don't think we in the United States have handled it very
well. Trade adjustment assistance is woefully inadequate, as

is the safety net for job losers more generally. We have done next to nothing to provide more job training or to adapt our K–12 educational system to the post-manufacturing age. Indeed, in public policy circles, we continue to bemoan the shrinkage of manufacturing jobs, to view it as a sign of failure, and to look for ways to arrest the process. Job losses in manufacturing industries have been fueling protectionist sentiment for decades. Frankly, I'd like to see us do better with the transition from impersonal service jobs to personal service jobs. Hence the clarion call.

Irwin and Lawrence are more sanguine about offshoring for other reasons as well. One, emphasized by Irwin, is that Indian (and other) suppliers of offshoring services will encounter rising supply prices as they attempt to hire more and more skilled workers. I agree with this proposition, but with heavy qualifications. Yes, skills—including good English-language skills—are in short supply in India, and wages in the offshoring sector are therefore rising rapidly. This is as it should be; it's part of the normal adjustment process that will narrow the wage gap between the United States and India. But Indian wages are still a fraction of U.S. wages for comparable jobs, and will remain so for decades. So the cost-saving motivation for offshoring will endure. Perhaps more important, India (and China, the Philippines, etc.) are not only *capable* of training tens (if not hundreds) of millions of additional workers for these jobs, *they are actually doing so*, as Richard Freeman reminds us in his comments.

Numbers matter, and they are staggering. Total U.S. employment is now about 140 million, and it is growing at less than 1 percent a year. The Bhagwati, Panagariya, and Srinivasan (2004, 108) guesstimate (quoted in my chapter) that India and China may add three hundred million skilled workers to the world's labor force over the next few decades suggests strong and continuing downward pressure on wages in tradable occupations, both here and in India. I'm no Malthusian, but I think rapid growth of the skilled work-forces of India and China will act as a strong check on wage increases there for a very long time to come.

Regarding wages in the United States, Lawrence disbe-lieves my regression that shows that, given education, the most offshorable occupations were already suffering notable wage penalties by 2004. I don't blame him; I'm skeptical myself. As I noted in the chapter, my prior belief was that I would find no such effect, and "it is hard to imagine that the mere threat of offshoring was having such large effects on wages by 2004" (p. 40). Lawrence may be right that the coefficient reflects some other influence (e.g., routinizabil-ity) that is not controlled in the regression. I welcome further research on this issue. Indeed, spurring such research was my main reason for publishing this provocative result in the first place.

Lawrence also chides me for (tacitly) advising Americans to prepare themselves for jobs in the nontradable sector (e.g., personal service jobs) rather than in tradables: "Advice to get out of the tradable sector may be quite wrong" (p. 6). Here I disagree. If I had school-age children now, I'd be advising them to prepare for careers in occupations that (a) a com-puter cannot do well, and (b) a well-educated Indian cannot do well. Some of these occupations will, I agree, be in U.S. export industries. But many more will be in personal ser-vices that cannot be offshored. If you don't want to make the sorts of sectoral bets that have given industrial policy a bad name ("This industry will win and that industry will lose"), the safer strategy is to head for the personal service hills.

Both Irwin and Lawrence, and also to some extent Bhagwati, are unimpressed by my policy recommendations. While they agree with the recommendations, they give me low marks for boldness and originality.[4] I plead guilty as charged. I am hardly the first, and won't be the last, to recommend more and better TAA, a thicker social safety net, more job retraining, improved education, and so forth. But as I said before, we are not really *doing* any of these things now. So the policy recommendations, boring as they are, bear repeating. Furthermore, I think I was at least *slightly* original, although admittedly light on specifics, in calling for changes in the *nature* of K–12 education—specifically, for more emphasis on the skill sets needed for careers in personal services, and less on the things computers and Indians can do well.[5] I take it from his comments that Lawrence, at least, would oppose such changes.

Next, let me deal briefly with Irwin's (undoubtedly correct) assertion that I cannot predict the future: "As he honestly and repeatedly admits, we are speculating about the future and we don't know how things are going to turn out. Could he be right? Sure! Could he be wrong? Yes, I think he would admit to that possibility" (p. 74).

I do admit to that possibility. I've long been a believer in the old saw "One thing you should never predict is the future." So why let valor triumph over discretion this time? I explained why early in the chapter (p. 24). If I am anywhere close to correct, forces are already in motion that will call for major (if boring) policy responses—the kinds of things that America's heavily checked and balanced system takes eons to accomplish. And in some cases, notably reform of the K–12 education system, the gestation periods are so long that it is already too late. To change the *outputs* of the K–12 system twenty years from now, we need to start changing the *inputs* (kindergarten education) seven years from now, which means we probably should have started debating the changes several years ago.

To me, but apparently not to Bhagwati, Irwin, or Lawrence, that means we must take a stab at *forecasting* the broad contours (though not, of course, the details) of the future, perilous as that may be. But is the task impossible? Maybe not. If I asked a bunch of economists to forecast the qualitative consequences of imposing a price ceiling of $30 a barrel on oil, I think few would hide behind their inability to foresee the future. Most would use elementary *theory* and would get it approximately (though not exactly) right. Similarly, my "forecast" of large increases in service offshoring is really based on only two premises: that ICT will keep improving, and that the skilled, English-speaking workforces of India, China, and other countries will continue to grow. Do I *know* for sure that these two things will happen? Of course not. But I think the odds are greatly in my favor. If these predictions prove correct, most of the rest of my scenario follows by the application of some pretty simple economic theory.[6]

Finally, let me end where I began—with opposition to protectionism. As noted earlier, Irwin casts me as the second coming of Ross Perot. In the same vein, Lawrence worries that my alarmist tone may "provoke the very protectionist responses that he says he'd like to avoid" (p. 92). I guess it's a judgment call, but in my judgment both discussants need a dose of reality.

According to Irwin, I am reawakening the "giant sucking sound" at a time when "one hears about this problem these days as [much as] one hears about the threat that Japan poses for the future livelihood of our children (p. 72)." Oh?

I suggest that Irwin turn on his television or open his newspaper. Every public opinion poll shows that support for free trade and globalization is ebbing. Outside the narrow community of economists (and a few fellow travelers), NAFTA is widely viewed as a failure. Democrats are falling over one another to decry it, revise it, or even repeal it. Republicans have turned so nativist that they remind me of nothing so much as the Know Nothings of the mid-nineteenth century. The Doha round has failed. May I humbly suggest that economists' tried-and-untrue strategies for defending free trade are not working so well?

What are the alternatives? Well, maybe we economists could start by admitting that trade expansions create both winners and losers. After all, we can't keep it secret—the losers already know it. Next, we could urge, and not as an afterthought, that more be done to ease the pain of the losers. Then, trade theorists in particular could start paying more attention to transitions and less to equilibrium states—which also points toward policies to ease the transitional pain (TAA, etc.). Finally, we could start putting in place policies that will facilitate the transition to a world in which large numbers of impersonal service jobs have been offshored. These are precisely the sorts of things I urge doing in my chapter. In my judgment, they constitute a far better way to defend free trade than stubbornly denying the obvious.

Response to Freeman and Kletzer

A response to the thoughtful discussions by Richard B. Freeman and Lori G. Kletzer is not really necessary, since the three of us are in near-total agreement. Just three quick points:

First, Kletzer (p. 84) is right; I misspoke about something. Laissez-faire is really *not* enough under the "business as usual" scenario because America does so little to help its displaced workers—whether displaced by trade or by anything else. Even if there were no such thing as electronic offshoring, we should still be doing much more to help the losers from industrial change.

Second, while the Jensen-Kletzer methodology for estimating offshorability and my own lead to similar overall numbers,[7] they differ in one important respect. In my estimates, education and offshorability are virtually uncorrelated; in theirs, the correlation is sizable (about +0.3). It would be useful to sort that out.

Third, I'd like to reiterate one of Freeman's criticisms of Bhagwati's chapter and relate it to a point I made earlier. Bhagwati writes as if disagreements among economists about the (gross vs. net) benefits of trade, as filtered through the news media, have profound effects on mass public opinion—which is why, in his view, people like me are dangerous. Freeman (p. 67) begs to differ: "Most Americans judge economic reality from what they observe in their lives, not from debates among economists or what journalists write. The reality includes job losses and threats of job losses due to offshoring and trade." I agree with Freeman, of course, which is why I think that recognizing the reality of non-Paretian trade—*and doing something about it*—is likely to do much more good than harm.

Notes

1. Lori Kletzer's discussion, unlike Bhagwati's, has this exactly right.

2. Irwin notes immediately after this sentence: "He would probably deny this charge." I do!

3. But that the gains outweigh the losses—which is the first lesson.

4. Freeman's recommendations are consistent with mine, but more radical. He also adds a few new ones, with which I mostly agree.

5. I elaborate on this theme in Alan Blinder, "Education for the Third Industrial Revolution," working paper for Urban Institute education project, February 2008.

6. As Freeman says (p. 2), "The doubling of the global labor force, investment in education in low wage countries, and digitalization of work seemingly makes offshoring inevitable."

7. Which does not mean that they are right!

References

Bhagwati, Jagdish N. 1968. "Distortions and Immiserizing Growth: A Generalization." *Review of Economic Studies* 35, no. 4: 481–485.

Bhagwati, Jagdish, Arvind Panagariya, and T. N. Srinivasan. 2004. "The Muddles over Outsourcing." *Journal of Economic Perspectives* 18, no. 4 (Fall): 93–114.

Samuelson, Paul A. 2004. "Where Ricardo and Mill Rebut and Confirm Arguments of Mainstream Economists Supporting Globalization." *Journal of Economic Perspectives* 18, no. 3 (Summer): 135–146.

Contributors

Jagdish Bhagwati
University Professor,
Economics and Law
Columbia University

Alan S. Blinder
Gordon S. Rentschler
Memorial Professor
Economics
Princeton University

Richard B. Freeman
Herbert S. Ascherman
Professor Economics
Harvard University

Benjamin M. Friedman
William Joseph Maier
Professor of Political
Economy
Harvard University

Douglas A. Irwin
Robert E. Maxwell '23
Professor of Arts and
Sciences
Dartmouth College

Lori G. Kletzer
Professor of Economics
University of California,
Santa Cruz

Robert Z. Lawrence
Albert L. Williams
Professor Trade and
Investment
Kennedy School of
Government
Harvard University

Index